Sinema7 brings faith into a mo... cinematic illustrations creates a fresh reflection of our own personal indulgences in light of those movies that subconsciously shape our behavior. Maureen Herring avoids the typical demonization of Hollywood prevalent in current Christian commentary by using an analytical approach to the characters, plots, and themes of these familiar stories. Rather than seeing movies as a constant threat to our culture's morality, her analysis sets the framework for a change in Christian worldview that creates a rich opportunity for the ideals of the Christian faith to become relevant in a world that often believes God is absent in our everyday lives. Sinema7 will alter the way that we approach entertainment and open the door for conversations with those who have lost sight of the greater glories of our faith.
-Rev. Stephen V. Allen

The structure and rhetorical execution in Sinema7 is top notch. It's a solid read, with great film quotes and vital, moral evaluations. Sinema7 is perfect courseware for a small group, and a great introduction to the questions of how we should live our lives. Any moral commentary that finds a way to reconfigure John Belushi's Bluto, from "Animal House," into a road sign for temperance ... is a commentary well-worth reading.
-Floyd Wray, author of *Blood Toys*

In Jesus' own ministry he did not shy away from honest discussion with those seeking eternal life... Through simple parables, he shared divine revelations. His ministry was unashamedly relevant—and so is this book.
-David McLain, Pastor, Bridge Community Church

SINEMA 7

A MOVIE WATCHER'S GUIDE TO THE SEVEN DEADLY SINS

Maureen Herring

Tabret Press Pflugerville, TX

© 2010 by Tabret Press

Published by Tabret Press, www.tabretpress.com
Pflugerville, TX

Printed in the United States of America

All rights reserved. No part of this publication may be reproduced, stored in a retrieval system, or transmitted in any form or by any means - for example, electronic, photocopy, recording - without the prior written permission of the publisher. The only exception is brief quotations in published reviews.

Library of Congress Cataloging-in-Publication Data
Herring, Maureen , 1958-
    Sinema7: how movies reveal the seven deadly sins in all of us / Maureen Herring.
           p.   cm.
    Includes bibliographical references and index.
    ISBN 978-0984-0959-02
    1. Motion pictures – Religious aspects. 2. Motion pictures – Moral and ethical aspects. 3. Deadly sins. 4. Sin – Christianity. I. Title.
PN1995.5 H34 2009
791.43   2009936614

Unless otherwise indicated, all Scripture quotations are taken from the Holy Bible, New Living Translation, copyright © 1996, 2004, 2007. Used by permission of Tyndale House Publishers, Inc., Carol Stream, Illinois 60188. All rights reserved.

Scripture quotations marked (NIV) are taken from the Holy Bible, New International Version®, NIV®. Copyright © 1973, 1978, 1984 by Biblica, Inc.™ Used by permission of Zondervan. All rights reserved worldwide.

Scripture taken from the New King James Version. Copyright © 1982 by Thomas Nelson, Inc. Used by permission. All rights reserved

Scripture taken from the NEW AMERICAN STANDARD BIBLE®, Copyright © 1960,1962,1963,1968,1971,1972,1973,1975,1977,1995 by The Lockman Foundation. Used by permission

Scripture taken from The Message. Copyright © 1993, 1994, 1995, 1996, 2000, 2001, 2002. Used by permission of NavPress Publishing Group.

*Thanks to my husband Ted.
I could not have written this book without
your encouragement, support, and editorial help.*

*Thanks to my sons, Eric, Nick, and Chad, and our friend
Drew for all the great playlist suggestions.*

*Thanks to my friends who took the time to read my
ramblings and give me feedback.*

Thanks to Jason and Mary Lou for the technical help.

You all rock.

TABLE OF CONTENTS

Introduction	1
Lust - *I want sex*	12
Gluttony - *I want food, booze, and drugs*	28
Greed - *I want more stuff*	42
Sloth - *I want nothing*	58
Anger - *I want to have my way*	72
Envy - *I want your stuff*	88
Pride - *I want to be better than you*	104
Conclusion	122
Appendix	131
Bibliography	158
Index	185

INTRODUCTION

"Tell me a story." Before we are old enough to read most of us have experienced many stories. Parents read to children before bed. Schools, churches, and libraries offer story times. We watch movies. We invent our own stories. They involve us intellectually, emotionally, spiritually, and even physically in a way mere statement of fact cannot. This is why teachers like Jesus and Aesop used stories. In our culture one of the most powerful ways that we experience stories is through movies. This book explores the seven deadly sins using tangible stories and relatable characters from movies that reflect how the sins play out in our culture.

Paul used the works of Greek philosophers to talk to the Greeks on Mars Hill (Acts 17) because they were familiar to the people he wanted to address. Paul understood that even though these works were not written by Jews or Christians, this literature contained truth that God had revealed. I believe many ideas expressed in movies reveal that there are some deeply held moral principles at work in our culture. This book is my attempt at applying Paul's "Mars Hill" approach to movies.

About the movies

Most movies, not just those we call dramas or epics, not just the critically acclaimed, but funny ones and even scary ones offer us glimpses into human needs and motivations. In this book we'll explore themes, characters, plots, and dialogue in a wide variety of movies, sometimes in depth and sometimes as a brief illustration. Since we're talking about the seven deadly sins, not all the movies discussed are what some might consider "family friendly." Sometimes profound searching can be found in what some might consider a "profane" story. A good story is going to challenge us, stretch us, and intrigue us, not just entertain us and affirm what we already think.

We will look at villains and heroes in movies as a means of examining our own predispositions toward sin and virtue. The very fact that most of us can identify the villains and heroes in a story and generally agree on a character's flaws and strengths says something about our common understanding of evil and good. People who would never label an action "sin" would identify characters like Hannibal Lecter, Catherine Tramell (*Basic Instinct*), Gordon Gekko, or Cruella de Vil as villains. We see wrath, lust, greed, and pride and recognize them as destructive forces in our world and destructive flaws in human nature.

The bad guys and the conflicts in the story are often what interest us most, and what we discuss most often. Evidently people, not just religious people but people in general, do want to talk about sin. It's part of our human condition. Movies offer a culturally relevant context in which to discuss sin. This provides opportunities for conversations about sin and redemption in which believers, seekers, or agnostics all get to feel like sinners.

Introduction

About sin and virtue

I have always found sin to be an awkward topic. Talking about it makes me feel like the church lady. We tend to think of sin as breaking rules of behavior. Ask any child "What are the rules?" and chances are that child will respond with a list of what he is not allowed to do. "No talking," "no running," "no hitting." Eight out of ten of the Bible's Ten Commandments are stated as "thou shall nots." Only "Keep the Sabbath" and "Honor thy father and mother" are stated as positives. Why is it that our grasp of what we are *not* supposed to do tends to be so much clearer?

Jesus came along thousands of years later and summarized all the rules as a positive with "Love the Lord your God with all your heart, all your soul, and all your mind... Love your neighbor as yourself. The entire law and all the demands of the prophets are based on these two commandments" (Matt. 22:37 - 40). The seven deadly sins are attitudes that counter this law of love. Ultimately sin is not about breaking the rules but about damaging souls and spirits, our own and those around us.

I believe using the seven deadly sins of lust, gluttony, greed, sloth, anger, envy, and pride presents sin to seekers, agnostics, Christians, and believers in other faiths in terms we can generally agree upon. Every one of the seven deadly sins is based on selfishness.

Storytellers use conflict in stories because often our selfishness kicks in and our flaws are revealed when we face conflict. Our actions and reactions seem to come from natural tendencies that feel like they are ingrained into our personalities. It is as if we are wired to react in a particular way to particular events. Christianity explains these tendencies as flaws that exist in our natures as a result of the existence of evil. The behavior that results from acting on these tendencies is called sin.

Acting on one of the seven deadly sins might initially make us feel more in control and more satisfied in the midst of whatever we're trying to deal with. We may turn our focus inward and yield to attitudes that seem to shield us from our sense of need. Or we may turn our focus outward and develop character traits that help us accept our needs, separate needs from desires, and look to the needs of others. We are not powerless; these are choices.

The opposing virtues are attitudes that adhere to the law of love. They represent those traits that do not come easily for those who struggle with a particular sin. Many movies present characters who seek to live in a more heroic way. Seeing how purity, discipline, generosity, passion, patience, kindness, and humility look in a story can help us to embrace change for ourselves and to explain redemption to others.

Perhaps experiencing someone else's journey in a movie can help us tell our own stories more effectively and remind us that they are important to tell. Many storytellers recognize how destructive these flaws can be and depict villains acting on their selfish tendencies and depict heroes with a longing to find freedom from selfishness. Often the characters in these stories mirror my own struggles. Seeing them from the omniscient perspective of a movie is helpful in gaining insight and compassion, and in finding inspiration for change.

About the book

Sinema7 is organized into seven chapters which present each one of the seven deadly sins and the virtue that opposes it. I chose movies and characters that best illustrate that sin

Introduction

to me. I also chose movie characters or quotes that seem to crop up as cultural references in conversations with others about movies, good and evil, and faith.

The appendix contains a history of the seven deadly sins for those interested in how this concept originated and evolved. There are also some lists of seven - 7 Bible verses, 7 movies, and 7 songs for each sin. Biblical references and movies discussed in each chapter are listed in the index.

No doubt you will think of many more movies you have seen that I did not mention. I've continued to write about movies and sin on my blog, and welcome ideas and input from others. Join the conversation at http://sinema7.net.

The following section is a brief explanation of "how to read a movie." It is intended to provide some background for those who may need a refresher on the elements of a story. It is also intended to enhance your future movie-watching experience and help you become skilled at gaining and sharing insight about the movies you enjoy and want to discuss. You are welcome to skip right to the sins.

How to read a movie

People who have seen the same movie connect with one another. If we are able to recognize how a movie presents truth we can go beyond just quoting lines and trading favorite scenes and engage in more meaningful conversation. In the context of a movie we can find a lot to say about the human condition, and about sin and redemption.

Literary analysis may have seemed deadly boring in 9th grade, but applying those principles to movie-watching can help us pull out the truths that are present in the story and use them to tell our own stories. Critics are people who study film, analyze movies, and then find entertaining ways to discuss the connections. We all have valuable and unique insights to add to this conversation.

Plots

Before movies were invented, before books and reading were widespread, there were storytellers. Some wove long elaborate stories that became legends. Some legends were set to music, becoming ballads. Homer's Odyssey and Beowulf (by the very prolific Anonymous) are good examples of these very old stories.

Other storytellers told short, pithy little tales in order to illustrate a point. Jesus and Aesop were masters of parables and fables respectively. Ancient cultures used legends, myths, fairy tales, fables, parables, and dramas to reveal human character and to describe abstract ideas.

Movies are the most popular way we tell stories at the beginning of the 21st century. In them we see ourselves and people we know. Universal ideas, personality types, and well-loved plots are presented to our generation as vividly as stories have ever been told.

Familiar tales are retold. Shakespeare's *Taming of the Shrew* becomes *10 Things I Hate About You*, and *Twelfth Night* becomes *She's the Man*. Jane Austen's *Emma* becomes *Clueless*. Homer's *Odyssey* becomes *O Brother Where Art Thou?*

New stories also express who we are as a culture, a subculture, or a generation. While some of the settings and ideas may seem unique to who we are right now, how a story is told is nothing new.

Some story plots are familiar because we have lived them. Anyone who has taken a family road trip can readily relate to *Little Miss Sunshine* or the *Vacation* movies! Some

Introduction

genres like science fiction or mob movies allow us to step into worlds we do not normally inhabit, yet the settings and characters are usually relatable in some way.

Characters

Just as they always have, characters flesh out experiences and emotions that are common to all of us. Regardless of setting, plot, or theme, characters are often age-old types that we recognize from other stories, or from our own acquaintances. We can identify the hero and the villain. We recognize whether characters are driven by motives that are honorable or selfish. In a good story with more than stock characters we may identify with a characters' internal struggle, external conflict, and personal growth.

Motive has everything to do with whether we see a character as redeemable. Often evil characters act out of desire for power, such as Sauron in *The Lord of the Rings*, or Lord Voldemort from the *Harry Potter* stories. Some villains seem motivated by greed, like *Die Hard's* Hans Gruber, or *Wall Street's* Gordon Gekko. While it is easy to admire the hero and despise the villains, characters who are more conflicted and display positive traits as they struggle with their darker inclinations are more realistic.

Every character comes with a set of tendencies that affect the story. Phil Connor in *Groundhog Day* is self-absorbed, vain, and inconsiderate, but redeemable. Connor experiences the same day over and over as he moves from making selfish choices to focusing on other people.

In *Groundhog Day* we actually see Phil Connors' tendencies change as he is able to identify and deal with issues that are affecting his relationships. Most of us can think of a day we wish we could do over. This movie is a pretty good picture of how spiritual discipline works. Attitude sometimes follows action, rather than the other way around. Eventually Phil Connors' others-centered choices become both voluntary and natural to him.

The teen cheerleader in *Buffy the Vampire Slayer* experiences a different sort of transformation. Her reaction to being told she is the "chosen one" is a little like Jonah's after God told him his next assignment was Nineveh. "Yeah, I'm the chosen one. And I choose to be shopping." Both characters have motives that counter their appointed tasks. Beneath the elements of horror and humor, *Buffy* is a story about embracing a mission in spite of the desire to satisfy self.

Will Munny in *Unforgiven* accepts a mission that proves destructive to his desire for redemption. He wants to believe his wife's influence has truly reformed him, but discovers that his violent nature is not really reconciled to the tenderness he has tried so hard to embrace. His is the conflict Paul the Apostle described in Romans 7:19: "I want to do what is good, but I don't. I don't want to do what is wrong, but I do it anyway." Characters like Will Munny break our hearts as their destructive spirals seem to move them farther and farther from redemption's path.

A character like Hannibal Lecter in *Silence of the Lambs* who demonstrates no visible resistance to evil seems unredeemable. He fascinates, perhaps even amuses, but ultimately repulses. In spite of how much evil may tempt us we are ultimately drawn to good, and usually root for redemption for characters we love.

Characters in stories help us gain a better understanding of ourselves and those around us. We do not have the benefit of an omniscient point of view when dealing with the people we encounter in our own lives. The Bible says that we "look on the outside but God looks on the heart" (1 Sam. 16:7b). We experience other people by what they do and say, by the results of their actions, by the way we feel when we are with them, and by comparing them with others. We can't know their motives. In stories we get a perspective on motives and tendencies that we seldom get as our own stories unfold in the living of our lives.

Theme

Every story uses plot, characters, and setting to present the theme, which is the main point of the storyteller. Sometimes the theme is a general idea like loyalty or courage. Sometimes there is a moral to the story, like "everyone has a role to play," a theme in *Lady in the Water*, or "liars will be found out," a theme in *The Tailor of Panama*.

Sometimes the theme is so obvious and heavy-handed in movies like *Lions for Lambs* that it hits us over the head with its political message at the expense of storytelling. Sometimes the theme is subtly woven into the story, such as in *Lost in Translation*. It is only after thinking about the story and processing it for awhile that we "get" what the filmmaker was saying.

We do not think of our real lives as having themes, plots, settings, and characters, but they do. We sometimes find ourselves in situations that seem to have implications for our future and the future of others. Sometimes the implications seem almost cosmic. As Sam said to Frodo in *The Two Towers*: "But that's not the way of it with the tales that really mattered, or the ones that stay in the mind. Folk seem to have been just landed in them, usually - their paths were laid that way, as you put it… I wonder what sort of a tale we've fallen into?…"

When we are in our own stories we are so involved in the action and setting that we don't always see our own characters fully or identify the themes in our own lives. But when we watch a movie we see the characters making the same mistakes over and over, and can easily identify their problems.

We may even identify some of our friends' issues by observing patterns of behavior. We know who we think of as "lucky" or "driven" or "vain." We all know people whose lives seem to be in a pattern of destructive relationships or overspending. We may try to tell them but they don't see it themselves, because they are so focused on the action, setting, and characters in their own stories that they fail to see the themes. The seven deadly sins weave their way into our stories, into our personalities and characters, and color the action, setting, and relationships in all our lives.

7 LUST

Are you not confusing love with lust? - William of Baskerville, *The Name of the Rose*

When love is for the highest bidder, there can be no trust. Without trust, there can be no love - Argentinean, *Moulin Rouge*

My understanding of women only goes as far as the pleasure. When it comes to the pain I'm like any other bloke - I don't want to know - *Alfie (1966)*

I search out the beauty that lies within until it overwhelms everything else. And then they cannot avoid their desire, to release that beauty and envelope me in it - *Don Juan De Marco*

Even before there was you, there was the promise of you - Abby McDeere, *The Firm*

I've had three lovers in the past four years, and they all ran a distant second to a good book and a warm bath - Dorothy, *Jerry Maguire*

You know, I cannot understand why the most sophisticated of women can't tell the difference between a meaningless, hot, passionate sexual affair and a nice, solid, tranquil, routine marriage - Harry Black, *Deconstructing Harry*

Lust

"I did not know there were seven deadly sins: please tell me the names of the other six" author Dorothy Sayers wrote of a conversation she once had with a young man. Often when we think "sin" we think "lust." Lust, like greed, gluttony, and envy, reflects personal dissatisfaction and a desire for more, or different experiences.

If we equate sexual satisfaction with feeding every sexual desire it might be hard to imagine life-long monogamy as sexually satisfying. In the 1979 version of *The In-Laws* a blindfolded Sheldon faces the firing squad, babbling "I've only had four women in my life. Two of them, my wife!" He regrets dying with so little sexual experience. We might see unknown sexual experiences as fun and exciting, while known experiences may seem routine.

In our culture lust has empowered an industry that caters to satisfying sexual desire without the commitment or intimacy. Lust can result in unfaithfulness, loss of virginity, prostitution, pornography, and uncommitted sex, all which seem to be common themes in many movies. Many of these movies are reflections of what we think love and sex are about.

Unfaithfulness

In *Moonstruck* Rose poses the question "Why do men cheat?" Rose knows her husband Cosmo is having an affair, and tries to understand why. After talking with several men she arrives at an answer: "Because they fear death."

Perry, a middle-aged professor Rose meets in a restaurant, tries to explain why he dates his students: "Sometimes I'm droning along and I look up… at a young woman's face, and see me there in her eyes, me the way I always wanted to be and maybe once was..." His lust is at least partially driven by his ego. It is also motivated by his desire to recapture the excitement and optimism of youth.

Fixation with youth accounts for part of Lester Burnham's mid-life crisis in *American Beauty*. He quits his job, buys a red convertible, and finds a job with the "least responsibility." Lester begins working out in his garage and lusting after his daughter's cheerleader friend Angela, who flirts with him. Lester misses the excitement and discovery of youth.

Much to his wife Carolyn's embarrassment, Lester abandons the corporate, materialistic, and social constraints that he believes have disconnected him. On the other hand Carolyn is no longer interested in intimacy, but with appearances. Lester has become a prop in her life rather than a partner. Carolyn's perfectionism sets up Lester to fail her, and sets her up to be disappointed in him.

For Lester, lust is a poor substitute for intimacy. Lester Burnham's solitary sexual gratification in the shower emphasizes his aloneness and need for intimacy. He tells us, "I have lost something. I'm not exactly sure what it is, but I know I didn't always feel this... sedated." Routine can suck the life out of living.

Lester has sexual fantasies about Angela because this is so much easier than doing the necessary work on his marriage to Carolyn. Carolyn starts an affair with someone who represents everything that she embraces and Lester rejects. She uses sex to affirm her lust for power, success, and image. She tells their daughter Jane, "You cannot count on anyone except yourself. It's sad, but true, and the sooner you learn it, the better." Perhaps Carolyn avoids intimacy with Lester because it makes her feel vulnerable.

Lester and Carolyn want uncommitted sexual encounters that simulate intimacy but do not require the emotional investment. Both transfer an image onto someone new to satisfy their fantasies and feed their egos. Perhaps unrealistic expectations are part of the reason we see sequential monogamy replacing lifetime commitments.

Values shift and couples often find themselves headed in different directions. Instead of talking about it we may hide who we really are from a spouse, because the person who can best offer support is also the most likely to hurt us. Sometimes the anonymity of lust looks safer and easier than the work involved in intimacy.

When Angela and Lester are eventually alone together he realizes "This is not the mythically carnal creature of [his] fantasies; this is a nervous child." Realizing how exposed she feels, Lester comforts her and tries to make her see that she is okay. By putting Angela's needs above his own Lester begins to see that intimacy requires responsibility for another person.

Intimacy can be more than physical. In *Lost in Translation* Bob and Charlotte meet in Tokyo, where neither speaks the language or totally understands the culture. This sort of situation can often bond people together, at least temporarily. Also, Bob seems to have a bit of an attitude that "what happens in Tokyo stays in Tokyo."

Charlotte confides that she's "stuck" in her marriage. Bob is honest and tells her it doesn't get any easier. Both Bob and Charlotte feel as if their marriages are becoming as unfamiliar and foreign as Tokyo, yet neither really wants to abandon their marriages.

Alienation and loneliness leads each to consider carrying their flirtation to the next level, but honest reflection reveals that neither is actually looking for sex so much as acceptance and openness. What they find in their friendship is the safe intimacy that each really hopes to rekindle in their marriages. More than anything each of them needs to feel valued and heard.

Eventually Bob is unfaithful to his wife, but not with Charlotte. He may have done this because he's allowed his attraction to Charlotte to build, but is determined not to sleep with her. Certainly he has compartmentalized sex and intimacy, but he doesn't see this. For him sex is just physical, while his bond with Charlotte is emotional. On top of that, he still loves his wife. Charlotte looks to Bob for wisdom in navigating a rough patch in her marriage and he lets her down. She is disappointed and angry with him.

Their relationship might be emotional adultery. Jesus challenges his followers, "But I say, anyone who even looks at a woman with lust has already committed adultery with her in his heart" (Matt. 5:28). Even when we don't follow through with sexual infidelity unfaithful hearts can cause painful rifts in our relationships.

In *Love Actually* Harry is tempted by his beautiful young secretary Mia. He feels complimented when she tells him at the company Christmas party, "I'll just be hanging round the mistletoe, hoping to be kissed." Harry doesn't do anything physical, but he is distancing himself from his wife Karen in his flirtation with Mia. Though Harry's marriage seems solid, having a beautiful younger woman find him attractive does something for Harry's ego that his wife's admiration cannot seem to spark.

Harry buys Mia an expensive necklace as a Christmas gift which Karen sees and thinks is for her. Karen is devastated when she finds a CD as her gift, instead of the necklace. The timing is wrong to address the issue, so she goes into their bedroom, sheds the tears she can't hold back, and then gains control for the kids' sake. This is what betrayal of trust looks like.

Eventually Karen confronts Harry, needing to know whether "it's just a necklace, or if it's sex and a necklace, or if worst of all it's a necklace and love?" Harry apologizes and is relieved to be able to say that "nothing happened." Something did happen, though. For Karen the necklace incident creates a situation in which life will "always be a little bit worse." Karen loves and forgives Harry, but emotional unfaithfulness has altered the comfort level of their relationship. There is uncertainty and insecurity in place of the trust that existed between them before.

The sex industry

Prostitution and pornography are considered "victimless." Many people do not consider these activities harmful. Looking at pornography, visiting strip clubs, and salivating over people with nice bodies in magazines or on the internet is considered normal behavior for men and, more and more, for women as well.

Based on the number of strip clubs that appear as settings in film one might conclude that men, especially policemen, go to strip clubs to have important conversations that have nothing to do with sex. *High Crimes, Exit Wounds, Beverly Hills Cop, Matchstick Men,* and *Independence Day* are just a few movies in which the strip club scenes seem a bit out of place and gratuitous. The plots of these movies did not really require a strip club setting.

Sex workers are often portrayed in movies as people with hearts of gold who are just in it for the money. *Pretty Woman* portrays a prostitute who ends up a princess. The stripper in *Independence Day* declares "I'm a dancer...

exotic. I don't mind, the money's good and my baby's worth it." *Trading Places'* Ophelia is an intelligent, compassionate prostitute whose plan for wealth involves "five more years on my back." The biographical film *Monster* explores an even darker side. Aileen Wuornos, a victim of rape and abuse, turns to prostitution at thirteen and murders her clients to pay for alcohol and hotel rooms for herself and her lesbian lover.

While money may be a factor in becoming involved in the sex industry, sexual abuse, drug addiction, or mental illness often figure into the decision. *Moulin Rouge* and *Leaving Las Vegas* portray a difficult and tragic lifestyle. Porn stars in *Boogie Nights* experience cocaine addiction, mental distress, and murder.

Many sex workers are victims. At the very least every prostitute and porn star is somebody's child. It is unlikely that anyone envisioned this future for his or her child. It is probable that someone's heart is broken over this choice. It is certain God's heart is broken.

Our spouses or future spouses are also victims when we allow our sexual expectations to be informed by the sex industry. If we come to believe that what we see on the screen is what we should expect in the bedroom we may never find sexual satisfaction in real life. Redirecting our desires toward a sexual fantasy represented by pornography or prostitution allows us to temporarily abandon our commitment to intimacy with our spouses. Lust becomes a habit that demands more and more to be satisfied.

Loss of virginity

There is an entire genre of "coming of age" movies such as *American Pie*, *Bad News Bears*, *Superbad*, and *Can't*

Hardly Wait which imply that losing virginity is an expected rite of passage for young people. It is oversimplification to equate "coming of age" with sex. "Coming of age" is a term for growing up or moving from ignorance to knowledge, or from innocence to experience. Sometimes it means moving toward maturity or realizing a truth.

As people make this transition in *Pleasantville* their lives move from black and white to color. Many of us have been taught to view a lack of sexual knowledge or experience as a negative. Jennifer, who is leading the charge for sexual awareness, discovers "I've had ten times as much sex as the others, how come I'm still black and white?" Experiencing sex does not make her self-aware or adult, although she sees sex as something that should achieve that end.

Color comes when characters become multi-dimensional. For some of the characters sexual experience is a part of that journey, but it is not the goal of the journey. For Jennifer it is the goal, thus, she may be sexually experienced but she remains incomplete and unfulfilled.

Bridget, in *The Sisterhood of the Traveling Pants*, really regrets losing her virginity. She likes an older boy and lets him know how she feels. Then she believes that she owes him sex since she flirted with him and led him on. Sometimes believing sex is a "social norm" can make us feel that sex is obligatory. It isn't.

In *The 40-Year Old Virgin* Andy's buddies are incredulous that he's never had sex. He's depicted as a geek who reads comic books and plays with action figures. While rather crude, *The 40-Year Old Virgin* makes Andy's friends' fixation with his virginity look pretty stupid. Andy seems pretty content while his friends measure their happiness by their sexual conquests. Knowing Andy actually causes his friends to rethink some of their shallow ideas about relationships.

Eventually one of his friends resorts to celibacy after a wrecked relationship.

Andy is an awkward guy, but, in spite of his friends' assumptions, having sex is unlikely to improve his social skills. He learns to have conversations with women by talking to them, not sleeping with them. Andy does not lose his virginity until marriage, though that isn't his intent. Sex is not the solution to Andy's social isolation.

Uncommitted sex

People often rush into physical intimacy at the expense of emotional intimacy, which is only safe in a committed relationship. In *The Wedding Singer* Robbie and Linda are engaged. Robbie is utterly invested in the idea of marriage. Linda obviously views engagement and marriage as separate commitments, since she leaves him at the altar.

A devastated Robbie can no longer enjoy singing at other people's weddings. He cries out, "Oh would somebody kill me please? Somebody kill me please." Perhaps the bond formed by an intimate physical relationship along with his expectation of commitment makes his heart more vulnerable.

Sex is supposed to be a bonding element in a relationship. An analogy might be that after using Super Glue™ to connect two items they won't separate cleanly. They end up torn or splintered. Breakups, after sex becomes involved, can leave both parties with ripped up spirits.

Robbie's friend Julia says, "I always just envisioned the right one being someone I could see myself growing old with." This is a vision of love that involves investing in one person for a lifetime. It implies the fidelity and commitment of marriage.

Purity

Purity, or chastity, is the virtue which opposes lust. Though some of us may take issue with how chastity is portrayed in many movies, some of those same movies provide valuable portrayals of purity and love. Beyond chastity, purity is an attitude about what being in a relationship means. It is letting go of selfishness and embracing the us-ness of being part of a couple. It is finding completion, friendship, romance, passion, and fidelity in a committed relationship.

In *A Walk to Remember* Jamie is committed to keeping her virginity. She doesn't come off as a prude, but as someone who is truly committed to her faith in Christ. She believes she is honoring her future husband by delaying sex until marriage.

Jamie experiences social rejection because of her stance, but her faith and attitude make a real impact on Landon. As their friendship turns into a romance Jamie asks Landon, "Are you trying to seduce me?" Landon replies, "Are you seducible?" She tells him she is not, to which he responds, "That's what I thought." Jamie's values influence Landon rather than the other way around.

Jamie and Landon hold hands, kiss, and take time to find out about one another. Their relationship culminates in marriage. Sex represents an important aspect of their union, not the union itself.

Completion

In *Jerry Maguire* Jerry and Dorothy struggle in Jerry's risky start-up business. As stress mounts Jerry seeks comfort and companionship from Dorothy. She falls for him, saying, "I love him! I love him for the man he wants to be. And I love him for the man he almost is."

Dorothy eventually realizes the openness and love that Jerry puts into his work is not translating into their marriage. "I have this great guy. And he loves my son. And he sure does like me a lot." She decides that being liked a lot is just not enough. Dorothy wants passion as well as companionship. She needs intimacy and she can't have it unless Jerry is utterly committed to loving her and building their relationship.

If we don't feel safe in our relationships we tend to hold back. We may retreat so that we can avoid being hurt. Jerry asks Dorothy, "What do you want, my soul?" Dorothy tells him, "I think I deserve that much." She's not looking for a 50/50 relationship, but for one that is 100/100.

Eventually Jerry appears at Dorothy's, declaring "I won't let you get rid of me. Tonight our little project has had a big night. But it wasn't complete. It wasn't nearly complete because you weren't there to spend it with me… I love you. You complete me." This is very much like Adam's declaration to Eve in the book of Genesis: "You are the bone from my bone and flesh from my flesh" (Gen. 3:23).

In many marriage ceremonies there is a reference to "the two are united into one" (Eph. 5:31). Often we associate this with physical union, sex, but it also refers to a spiritual and emotional union. Two individuals become a new and separate entity, a couple, in which each is completely invested on a spiritual, emotional, and practical level.

This isn't to say couples lose their identities as individuals, but that we are so honest and connected and vulnerable with one another that we really do complete one another. Most of us aren't even close to that sort of connectedness, but it's more than a romantic notion. It is the sort of relationship we were created to enjoy.

Friendship

When Harry Met Sally explores whether men and women can ever be just friends. After many years of being "just friends" Harry goes over to comfort Sally when she discovers that her ex-fiancé is getting married. She's vulnerable and close, and before he knows it he's kissing her. In the next scene they are lying in bed. Sally is asleep, smiling. Harry looks confused and terrified.

The next morning Harry calls his friend Jess, "It's just like most of the time you go to bed with someone, she tells you her stories, you tell her your stories. But with Sally and me, we've already heard each other's stories, so once we went to bed, we didn't know what we were supposed to do, you know?... I don't know. Maybe you get to a certain point in the relationship where it's just too late to have sex, you know?"

Harry makes the all too familiar assumption that familiarity decreases desire. He buys in to the idea that sex with a relative stranger is more intriguing. The idea is that once a couple finds out what one another is like in bed the mystery is over, and it's time to move on. Eventually Harry realizes that it is that very familiarity that makes him love Sally so much.

Throughout the movie are short interviews with couples who have been married for a long time. Many of these people are really quirky. Sometimes one of the spouses looks at the other one like he or she is just insane, but the affection and friendship in their relationships is evident.

Romance

Not only do we need friendship, we need romance. *The Princess Bride* is a fairy tale love story. There is lots of sword fighting, great humor, and a decidedly romantic take on love. Westley declares to Buttercup, "This is true love. Think this happens every day?" After a series of challenging events in which they prove their love for one another, Westley and Buttercup kiss. "Since the invention of the kiss there have been five kisses that were rated the most passionate, the most pure. This one left them all behind."

Perhaps we are touched by romance in film because we are meant to be romantics when it comes to our spouses. Romance means that we look at our love as something that doesn't happen every day. Romance is an antidote to lust.

Passion

Earlier we looked at a subplot in *Moonstruck,* Rose's quest to understand adultery. The main plot of the movie involves Rose's daughter Loretta and her struggle between reason and passion. She agrees to marry Johnny because she's afraid of being alone, and because Johnny fits into the neat, safe, predictable life she envisions for herself. When she meets Johnny's brother Ronny she realizes that passion is still possible, but that it isn't safe. Loretta resists, explaining, "Maybe my nature does draw me to you, but I don't have ta go with that. I can take hold of myself and say yes to some things and no to something that's just gonna ruin everything! I can do that."

Loretta has self-control and logical thinking down pat. While these are indeed traits that help us to avoid lust, they are not intended to cause us to avoid love and passion as well. Passionate Ronny believes love "don't make things nice - it ruins everything. It breaks your heart. It makes things a mess… We are here to ruin ourselves and to break our hearts and love the wrong people and die."

Entering into intimacy requires a willingness to have our fantasies ruined and our hearts broken. Love is risky. Imperfection makes all of us the "wrong" people. Passion gives us permission to risk our hearts, while commitment and fidelity make it a little safer.

We find balance in Rita and Raymond, who are Loretta's aunt and uncle. They are always seen together as a couple. Their relationship is both practical and passionate. They've been married for many years, and to them "marriage is happy news." Like many older couples he's sort of pudgy and bald; she has a few extra chins. Not the typical, sexy movie couple we normally witness in a bedroom scene. Yet when the moon shines into their bedroom the years together do not mean the end of romance.

When Raymond flirts with his wife in their store, Rita says "Shut up. They'll hear you in the back." To which Raymond replies, "So what? The pleasure of marriage is you sleep with the woman and then you don't worry about nothing. Hey, how about a date tonight, Rita. Let's eat pasta and roll around." A marriage in which "you don't worry about nothing" is indeed an emotionally safe and physically satisfying experience.

Embracing purity and resisting lust doesn't mean becoming a prude or wearing a chastity belt. Single people, like Jamie, can decide that we are not seducible before we ever find ourselves in a tempting situation. We can control lust by knowing ourselves and carefully choosing what we watch and read, if those things are catalysts for sexual gratification. Sometimes we are drawn to movies about romance and sex because it turns us on, and sometimes it's because we're longing for passion and romance in our own lives.

Embracing purity means rethinking what we think sexual relationships are meant to be. As with every one of the seven deadly sins, the bottom line is selfishness. Lust is about self gratification, while sexual intimacy is an expression of love between two people. Sex definitely should involve pleasure, but the focus should be the other person's pleasure. Love seeks to satisfy rather than demanding satisfaction. Instead of compartmentalizing sex and love we can allow them to meld into something unique and special that is part of the us-ness of being a couple.

7 GLUTTONY

Fat, drunk, and stupid is no way to go through life, son - Dean Wormer, *Animal House*

Nothing exceeds like excess - Elvira Hancock, *Scarface*

Did he just say big, fat pig?... Do you think he meant me? - Caesar, *History of the World Part 1*

Beer... Now there's a temporary solution - Homer Simpson, *The Simpsons*

I believe in excess - Jim Morrison, *The Doors*

We don't sell Tic Tacs, we sell cigarettes. And they're cool, available, and addictive. The job is almost done for us - BR, *Thank You For Smoking*

Me want cookie! - The Cookie Monster, *Sesame Street*

Gluttony

Gluttony can be rather difficult to hide. Those of us who engage in it are often easy to spot, which makes Overeater's Anonymous a somewhat ironic name. We can develop the same passion for other substances that we can for food. Those excesses may not show up as girth, but usually take their toll on the body nonetheless. So whether we are epicureans, junk food junkies, beer guzzlers, or midnight tokers, that unreasonable, excessive devotion we have toward the substances we consume into our bodies is gluttony.

Obese people know they are fat. Addicts know they are hooked. Denial happens to those who are in the process of developing the habit of excess. In *Traffic* Judge Wakefield is up for appointment as America's next "drug czar," while his daughter Caroline is being turned on to crack cocaine by friends at her exclusive private school. Her boyfriend Seth explains to the shocked Judge, "I can stop, you know. I can stop. But she... cannot. You know, for me, it's like a weekend thing... but for her... it's different." Nobody plans to develop dependence on food, alcohol, tobacco, or drugs. Habits, even dependencies can be formed when occasional indulgences are repeated with increasing frequency by people who are pretty sure it's just "a weekend thing."

We do not usually think about why we like eating or drinking or smoking, we just know we feel better when we indulge. Then we overindulge, thinking we'll feel better still. We may overindulge because we're bored or stressed. Sometimes low self-esteem is both the reason and result of gluttony. These substances offer instant gratification when we need comfort. We can use food or other substances to relieve anxiety or receive comfort. Food, smoking, drugs, or alcohol become adult pacifiers.

Gluttony

Overindulgence

In a memorable scene from *Animal House* Bluto eats his way through the cafeteria food line and then sits down at a table where his table mates are told to "just keep your hands and feet away from his mouth." Some of us eat because we like food; some of us eat because we like eating.

In *Austin Powers: The Spy Who Shagged Me* Fat Bastard laments, "Do ya have tae call me fat? I tried going on a diet ye know... But the portions were so wee I ate the delivery man." Many of us extend the pleasure of eating well beyond the point at which we feel full. We can find quick and easy satisfaction in eating and allow it to become an emotional crutch. Eating becomes the focus rather than the food itself.

In *Super Size Me* Spurlock conducts an experiment in which he eats 3 McDonald's meals a day, for a month. If they ask him whether he wants to super size he must say "yes." He gains almost 25 pounds, ups his cholesterol, and damages his liver. In the film Spurlock says that obesity is now the second most preventable cause of death in the United States. Smoking is first. The primary message of *Super Size Me* is that each one of us needs to take some responsibility for our eating habits.

Snobbery

While some of us eat mass quantities indiscriminately, there are others who are quite discriminating. For these people it's all about the food. Today we call them "gourmands" or "foodies." Thomas Aquinas called them "sumptuous eaters." Some of us are really hard to feed. We reject or criticize food we consider sub-par. We can become so focused on quality that we become food snobs.

Remy, the main character in *Ratatouille*, enjoys fine dining while the rest of his family is content to eat garbage. Only a sumptuous eater like Remy would say something like "Are you detecting a certain oaky nuttiness?"

Ratatouille is full of gourmands. All the cooks qualify, but Anton Ego, the food critic, is the ultimate illustration of this. He strikes fear in the hearts of chefs because he visits restaurants in hopes of finding a mistake. He says, "After reading a lot of overheated puffery about your new cook, you know what I'm craving? A little perspective. That's it. I'd like some fresh, clear, well seasoned perspective." Ego has become such a food snob that he seldom enjoys anything he eats.

In contrast to the "sumptuous eaters" there are "ravenous eaters," those we traditionally consider gluttons who eat a lot, and usually eat it quickly. Remy's ravenous brother Emile plows into a delicacy Remy has prepared, only to be told "No, no. Don't just hork it down!" Emile isn't interested in quality or manners. As a ravenous eater Emile does not take the time to really enjoy his food or experience mealtime. As a gourmand Remy cares about quality, and wants his family and friends to enjoy the food he's prepared.

Mealtime is supposed to be a time to celebrate our blessings and nourish our bodies. It is a time to recharge and connect. Good food is supposed to be part of that experience, but it is not supposed to *be* the experience.

Boredom

In *Sideways* Miles' passion and meaning are wrapped up in wines. He's a divorced, unpublished author who teaches

Jr. High School English. He is on his way to becoming an alcoholic. Miles' preoccupation with wine is his way of compensating for boredom and disappointment. He may feel uninspired in other areas of his life, but wine engages his mind and his senses.

To celebrate his friend Jack's upcoming marriage Miles and Jack take a road trip into California's wine country to golf and drink. When Jack cheats on his fiancé Miles tries unsuccessfully to get him to be faithful. Jack notices Miles' alcoholism and depression, and does what he can to intervene. Yet neither man can see his own excesses.

When Miles meets Maya, who shares his appreciation of wine, he describes his favorite wine, Pinot Noir, as "quirky, vulnerable, and haunting." For Miles the personalities of wines are more approachable and less threatening than the personalities of people. His obsession with wine gives him a sense of accomplishment that substitutes for finishing his book, finding love, and everything else he's afraid to do with his life.

Self-destructive behavior

For some, what starts out as coping behavior escalates into an out-of-control, self-destructive fixation on the substance. In *Leaving Las Vegas* Ben Sanderson begins drinking heavily after his wife takes their son and leaves. He loses his job because of his drinking as well. Ben gets the shakes at the bank and has to leave and get a drink before he can go back and cash his severance check. Then he burns everything he owns, severs all ties, and moves to Las Vegas, determined to drink himself to death.

Moving to Las Vegas, Ben meets Sera who asks whether "drinking is a way of killing yourself?" Ben replies that "killing myself is a way of drinking." Eventually Ben and Sera, who is a prostitute, move in together with the agreement that they will not intervene in each others choices. He tells Sera, "You must never ask me to stop drinking."

Ben and Sera's attempts to develop any sort of really supportive relationship are derailed by Ben's escalating addiction and the unwillingness of both to let go of their destructive lifestyles. Ben moves out. Sera eventually finds Ben and tries to love him on his own selfish terms.

Sera continues on her own self-destructive path, despite witnessing Ben's downward spiral. *Leaving Las Vegas* is like a tragic opera that is both appalling and heartbreaking. It is a reminder that some lifestyle choices marginalize people who want hope and relationship as desperately as anyone.

We are sometimes so careful about maintaining personal space that our boundaries can become walls. Perhaps we should all be more willing to intervene, more willing to open our arms to someone in emotional pain, and more willing to walk into open arms when we are experiencing pain.

Addiction

In Monty Python's *The Meaning of Life* there is a scene in a restaurant involving an extremely large man. He has ravenously eaten a massive meal, much to the disgust of those sitting around him. The waiter has brought the check and offers him a mint. He refuses. The waiter persists, dismissing it as "just one thin mint," until the man finally eats the mint and explodes. Addiction works like that one thin mint. Knowing we've had enough, we want just one more. We avoid considering that one more will someday be one too many.

Gluttony

In *28 Days* Gwen Cummings gets drunk, trashes her sister's wedding, and wrecks a limo. She's had a drinking problem for some time but won't admit it. Her sister and the judge offer rehab or jail.

Gwen doesn't want to cooperate with the rules at rehab, and finds the touchy-feely group meetings uncomfortable and silly. She sees other people in rehab as stereotypical addicts and doesn't think she belongs there. Eventually Gwen admits that she is not better than any of them.

At one point Gwen's boyfriend Jasper visits her in rehab and brings her alcohol. He justifies it, saying, "The whole point of the game is to minimize the pain. People are born, they have a limited amount of time going around thinking life is dandy but then, inevitably, tragedy strikes and they realize life equals loss!" When we hurt we want to feel better. Walking through the pain and waiting for relief are counterintuitive for those who use substances to provide a way to feel better right now.

Gwen decides to walk through the pain. She is willing to do what it takes to change, even though she doesn't feel entirely accommodated by the rehab methods. The sober Gwen doesn't feel like the person she's comfortable being. She must trade instant relief for an undefined period of adjustment. *28 Days* ends with uncertainty about Gwen's future because her sobriety really is a day by day decision.

Obesity

In the deleted scenes from *Super Size Me* Morgan Spurlock speaks with members of Overeaters Anonymous. While many speak about the comfort they find in food, others indicate that the social stigma associated with being fat contributes to their continued overeating. One expert says that in any society where there are unrealistic expectations concerning body image, not only do eating disorders skyrocket, but so does obesity.

In *Heavy Weights* kids at a fat camp are humiliated and bullied by camp director Tony Perkis and his staff. Many of the kids in this movie have a hard time confronting people. They use food to stuff those words back in.

At one point the kids enjoy a gluttonous evening of gorging and wallowing in food. The next morning kids lie groaning in puddles of chocolate and ketchup. A sympathetic counselor, who is also overweight, tells them that they need to become healthy for themselves, not because their weight embarrasses someone else. He tells them that they are worthwhile and important.

What's Eating Gilbert Grape offers a compassionate look at how Bonnie Grape's daily choices about food result in an overwhelming condition that affects every member of the family. Gilbert feels trapped. His mother Bonnie has become so large that she cannot take care of the house or his mentally challenged brother. She cannot climb the stairs to her bedroom. She's uncomfortable going out in public. She has a limited wardrobe. She has become a burden to her children. Obesity shrinks her world.

We do not know all of Bonnie's issues, but we do discover that her husband has disappeared. Bonnie is experiencing valid feelings of pain and loss that need to be addressed. Instead of dealing with her issues, she eats.

After we've overindulged we experience temporary pleasure, but whatever was driving us to overindulge is probably still there. Now we not only have that issue to face but also the frustration and guilt we may feel due to overindulging.

Bonnie hates herself for becoming so fat, but she also hates everyone else for rejecting her for being fat. We only add to the baggage when we attach social stigma to an already difficult problem. Addictions are baggage, weights that prevent us from living the unique lives God has given each of us to live. Paul writes "Let us strip off every weight that slows us down, especially the sin that so easily trips us up. And let us run with endurance the race God has set before us" (Heb. 12:1b). It is so much easier to run when those around us are encouraging us.

Self-control

Self-control involves moderation, persistence, and endurance. It also challenges us to find appropriate ways to deal with life issues without depending on a substance for comfort. When we feel angry, depressed, worried, inadequate, bored, or lonely we can pray about it, talk about it, solve it, or get over it rather than trying to drink, eat, or smoke it away.

Self-control is not about self-denial but about behavior that stems from a change of heart as well as a change of habit. Gluttony only sees enjoyment while asceticism tends to see only nourishment. Addicts need complete abstinence, but this isn't an option for food addicts. Once we've decided to change our habits we can learn self-control and moderation, or we can overcompensate and place an equally excessive focus on our new discipline. This is gluttony too.

Moderation

Paul wrote to the Colossians about merely following dietary rules as a discipline: "These rules may seem wise because they require strong devotion, pious self-denial, and severe bodily discipline. But they provide no help in conquering a person's evil desires" (Col 2:23). C. S. Lewis explained that "in the days when the second Cardinal virtue was christened "Temperance" it... referred not specially to drink, but to all pleasures; and it meant not abstaining, but going the right length and no further." Over-indulgence and over-discipline are both self-centered pursuits. It is up to us to find that temperate yet tasty middle ground.

Chocolat is about temperance rather than abstinence. Just as Lent begins, Vianne opens a chocolate store right across the street from the church in a small town in France. The Mayor Comte Paul de Reynaud sees Vianne's shop as an affront to Lent, and chocolate as a carnal indulgence.

Paul is legalistic and extremely disciplined. He wants everyone in the community to do what is expected and follow all the rules. Paul tries to manipulate Pere Henri, the new young priest, who is trying to honor the expectations of the community. Paul goes so far as to write sermons for Pere Henri.

As each person chooses to enter the shop, Vianne makes individual chocolate recommendations. Though Vianne is dealing with some extreme baggage of her own, she cares about her customers and becomes involved in their lives. Each customer's life changes for the better after meeting Vianne.

Villagers come to Pere Henri to confess. They are conflicted because they assume that eating the chocolate is sinful, yet they are experiencing a joy in their lives that was missing before. Pere Henri writes his own sermon at last, "I think that we can't go around... measuring our goodness by what we don't do. By what we deny ourselves, what we resist, and who we exclude." Legalism is not the same as self-control. The patrons in *Chocolat* enjoy their chocolate but don't overindulge in it.

In *Willie Wonka and the Chocolate Factory* chubby Augustus Gloop dives into a river of chocolate as the Oompa Loompas sing, "What do you get when you guzzle down sweets, eating as much as an elephant eats, what are you at, getting terribly fat, what do you think will come of that?"

Their message is the same as Proverbs 25:16 which says, "When you're given a box of candy, don't gulp it all down; eat too much chocolate and you'll make yourself sick" (Message Bible). It doesn't say not to eat the chocolate; it says not to eat too much. Moderation involves figuring how much is "enough," rather than "too much."

Persistence

Rudy demonstrates the persistence and discipline necessary for self-control. Rudy has a dream to play football at Notre Dame. He spends four years working in a plant and two years at Jr. College, applying to Notre Dame each semester and being rejected. After being accepted he tries out for the football team and gets on the practice squad, not because of his athleticism but because he shows such heart.

Rudy focuses each day on the tasks that will lead to fulfilling his dream. Each day he studies, attends class, works out, goes to work, and shows up for practice. There is no guarantee that he will ever see a real game. Years after he begins doing what it takes to make his dream a reality, Rudy plays the last few seconds of the last game of his senior year.

In the 9th chapter of I Corinthians Paul notes the discipline it takes to compete in sports. He recommends this discipline as a way to develop self-control. Perhaps those of us who are prone to overindulgence might want to consider taking up a sport.

Persistence means long term commitment. If we are giving up pasta or chocolate or beer today we want to wake up thinner tomorrow. Regardless of promises on late-night TV, most of us will not drop three sizes in a week. We are used to the instant gratification we receive from our substances of choice, and we want our results instantly as well. In the Bible the writer of Hebrews says that "no discipline is enjoyable while it is happening. It's painful" (Heb 12:11).

Endurance

Former smokers, recovering alcoholics, and drug users will probably still describe themselves as addicts. The desire to indulge again never really leaves. We may continue to connect a substance with satisfaction even though we've cut down or quit.

Feeling "normal" without our substance of choice may take some time. Alcoholics Anonymous uses the slogan "one day at a time." Self-control is very much a one day at a time deal. We may mess up and have to start over.

In *Tender Mercies* Mac, a recovering alcoholic songwriter, encounters Rosa Lee, who provides him with acceptance and unconditional love. At one point he faces a stressful experience and buys a bottle of whiskey. Though he doesn't drink it, his response to his problem is to look for consolation there.

As their relationship progresses Mac responds to Rosa Lee's faith in him and in Christ. She not only believes in the transformative power of Christ, but she has faith in Mac's

Gluttony

ability to experience that transformative power. Mac's source of consolation shifts.

Near the end of the movie a devastating event tries Mac's faith. He is faced with one of the big questions in life: why God allows tragedy. He says "I don't trust happiness. I never did, I never will." His response this time though is to move on, without using alcohol to numb the pain. Without an answer, carrying his grief, Mac finds consolation in faith and love.

Gratification

Substances often serve as substitutes, instant gratification when we feel needy. Our hope is to discover gratification that is real and lasting, if not instant. We will always face stressful situations. We all have choices about what we dwell on and about how we handle it.

The Message Bible puts it like this: "If you decide for God, living a life of God-worship, it follows that you don't fuss about what's on the table at mealtimes or whether the clothes in your closet are in fashion. There is far more to your life than the food you put in your stomach, more to your outer appearance than the clothes you hang on your body. Look at the birds, free and unfettered, not tied down to a job description, careless in the care of God. And you count far more to him than birds" (Matt 6:26).

We legitimately do need relief and comfort. How we seek His comfort and become "careless in the care of God" is a life-long journey. Part of that journey is letting go of temporary emotional fixes so we can experience the true source of consolation for which gluttony is a mere substitute.

7 GREED

Greed, for lack of a better word, is good. Greed is right. Greed works. Greed clarifies, cuts through, and captures the essence of the evolutionary spirit - Gordon Gekko, *Wall Street*

Rule number one: don't underestimate the other guy's greed - Frank, *Scarface*

Mother always said you were greedy. She meant it as a compliment - Randolph Duke, *Trading Places*

Show me the money! - Rod Tidwell, *Jerry Maguire*

Well I see them. I see 50,000 men brought here to fight for one man's greed - Hector, *Troy*

It doesn't matter if you're black or white (money is falling all around). The only color that really matters is green - Peter Griffin, *Family Guy*

Great kings of men, but Sauron the Deceiver gave them nine rings of power, and, blinded by their greed, they took them without question, one by one falling into darkness - Galadriel, *Fellowship of the Ring*

Greed

In the iconic scene from *The Jerk* a dejected Navin Johnson shuffles down the sidewalk, declaring "All I need is this ashtray... and this paddle game... The ashtray, this paddle game, and the remote control, and the lamp, and that's all I need." He keeps repeating the list, adding more and more things that he just has to have in order to feel better. Sometimes we use our possessions to fill empty places in our lives and hearts that material items were not intended to fill.

Recognizing the dangers of greed, nearly every religion speaks against it. For Buddhists greed is one of three poisons. Identifying greed as one of the primary causes of suffering in the world, one of their dharmas of Hinduism is to avoid greed. In order to avoid greed Muslims pay a mandatory donation to charity, called a Zakat, to observe one of the five pillars of Islam. Jewish teaching identifies greed as a lack of trust in God.

Christianity teaches that greed creates discontent, and is a motivation for much evil. "You desire and do not have; so you kill. And you covet and cannot obtain; so you fight and wage war. You do not have, because you do not ask. You ask and do not receive, because you ask wrongly, to spend it on your passions." (James 4:1-3).

Greed is about the reasons we want, rather than about what we have. We acquire money and the stuff it buys for all sorts of reasons. Owning a great home, driving a nice car, and having a healthy bank account all feed the ego. Status comes with wealth. Having enough makes us feel more secure. Our possessions can make us feel more acceptable to others. Some of us just accumulate out of sheer materialism, because we can afford it. We like what we see and just want to own it. We feel the desire to have more and believe that having more will make us happier.

Money as status

Real life stock market trader Ivan Boesky said, "Greed is all right, by the way... I think greed is healthy. You can be greedy and still feel good about yourself." This attitude is mirrored in the movie *Wall Street* by the character Gordon Gekko. His speech to a room full of stockholders has become a defining moment in film. "The point is, ladies and gentlemen, that greed, for lack of a better word, is good. Greed is right. Greed works. Greed clarifies, cuts through, and captures the essence of the evolutionary spirit. Greed, in all of its forms - greed for life, for money, knowledge - has marked the upward surge of mankind..." Gekko's greed is tied to personal success and worth.

For Gekko, "if it's worth doing it's worth doing for money" and he is not interested in how his profit affects other people. Gekko believes that greed is a motivator for success, and success is a valid method of measuring human worth. Indeed for Gekko the thrill is not only in making money, but in winding up on the top of the pile. Defeating others in the process of corporate takeovers adds feelings of power and status to the satisfaction he experiences in making more money.

Young trader Bud Fox, attracted to the money and power, seeks to become Gekko's protégé. In his quest for success Fox is willing to trade his integrity, his relationships, and his family's financial stability to gain the lifestyle and excitement that his alliance with Gekko offers him. This movie has become a classic study in the culture of corporate greed in the 1980's. Capitalism is not inherently evil but it can create an environment that inspires unbridled greed in some people.

Status is the motivation behind ostentatious materialism. Mad Magazine once stated that "The only reason a great many American families don't own an elephant is that they have never been offered an elephant for a dollar down and easy weekly payments." Nowhere are status items so publicly discussed as in the television show *Cribs*.

Cribs provides an opportunity for greed, pride, and envy to converge as rich celebrities have an opportunity to exhibit their expensive possessions so that those watching at home can wish all that great stuff belonged to them. Entertainers and sports figures sometimes experience almost instantaneous wealth. Unfortunately common sense and compassion are not enclosed with that first big paycheck. Many overspend and invest in themselves, believing their own hype. They buy in to the myth that financial worth is a reflection of personal worth.

Money as security

In *Fargo* Jerry Lundergard wants money so that he can gain independence from his overbearing employer and father-in-law Wade. Jerry believes money will make him worthy, both in his own eyes and in the eyes of his wife and son. When Jerry brings Wade a financial opportunity he says, "This could work out real good for me and Jean and Scotty." Wade's response that "Jean and Scotty'll never have to worry" does not do much to help Jerry feel secure. If Jerry hopes to earn Wade's or Jean's respect he must demonstrate his financial prowess. Jerry has a nice home and makes a decent living, but he is motivated by greed mixed with pride and fear. Jerry is greedy for the freedom, security, and status that money can provide.

Greed

For many of us it's not the material things that money can buy, but the freedom from worry and control that attracts us. So much of our time and energy is spent doing things other people dictate, and earning money to pay for taxes and necessities. Money is the commodity that can buy us time for ourselves and power over our circumstances. Rather than seeking fulfillment in our present circumstances we focus on our dissatisfaction and insecurity. We see money as the agent of change.

In his quest for money Jerry hatches what he believes is a fool-proof plan to solve his money woes. He hires Gaear Grimsrud and Carl Showalter to kidnap his wife, with the idea that they will split the money. Finally, Wade insists on delivering the money himself. When Jerry tries to dissuade him he tells him, "Look, Jerry, you're not selling me a damn car. It's my show here." Jerry believes that unless he gets the money it will never be his show.

One scene shows Jerry sitting in his office dealing with the realization that he will be found out. The camera and lighting make the vertical blinds in his office look like a prison bars. Jerry's greed has imprisoned him.

The police officer Marge operates outside insecurity and greed. When Marge's husband Norm wins a contest that puts his art on a stamp he is frustrated that it wasn't more than a 3 cent stamp, while Marge rejoices that he's received the recognition. Marge's attitude is accepting and joyful, "That's terrific... I'm so proud of ya, Norm. Heck, Norm, you know we're doin' pretty good."

In America and in many other nations as well, most of us are "doing pretty good." Some of us have a tendency to be unsatisfied with what we have. We may think we need the newest generation of every electronic gadget or the latest and greatest car. No matter how much we have, something in us always wants more.

Marge later contemplates the death and devastation that greed has brought, saying, "And for what? For a little bit of money. There's more to life than a little money, you know." Marge understands the concept of enough. Rather than constantly striving for more than she has, she allows little encounters throughout her day to feed her sense of contentment. Marge's security and satisfaction is a stark contrast to Jerry's fearful greediness. In Jerry, *Fargo* presents an extreme example of a man who sees money as both security and hope.

Many of us want more than we have. Some of us are more motivated by fear of loss. We buy lots of insurance and try to squirrel away a nest egg. Frugality can come from a sense of responsibility and stewardship, but it can also stem from fear. We do whatever we can to hang on to what we have, and are constantly afraid we might lose it. Money is security, and we are less comfortable with risk.

Others tend to see money as hope. People on the hope end of the continuum buy lottery tickets and join MLMs. We fear that things will never change unless we take some sort of action. We are willing to take a certain amount of risk in order to improve our lot.

Money as hope

Las Vegas may be the capital city of greed. People dream of the big score and that dream keeps people gambling. If we can't win it like Rusty Griswold in *Vegas Vacation* maybe we can cheat and win like Charlie Babbitt attempts to do in *Rain Man*. Charlie kidnaps his autistic brother Ray in order to obtain control of their dad's inheritance. After discovering Ray's savant talent for counting cards Charlie

Greed

heads for Vegas willing to cash in at his brother's expense. Charlie puts his own greed above his brother's needs.

An entire industry built on greed is likely to be run by some greedy people, as demonstrated in *Oceans Eleven*. First made in 1960 and again in 2001, in *Oceans Eleven* greedy people outwit and steal from unlikable and even greedier people. Somehow robbing a casino doesn't actually seem like stealing, and this gives the audience permission to wholeheartedly root for the thieves.

Stories about unexpected windfalls are part of our culture. Many of us share a daydream about winning the lottery or finding money that, for perfectly legitimate reasons, is impossible to return. If we happen to come into the money most of us have significant plans for it. We might dream of getting out of debt or taking a vacation. We think of all sorts of ways we might improve our lives and those of our families and friends, if we just had the money. We could afford to be charitable. Most of us believe we would be responsible and worthy stewards should a bag of money land in our laps.

In *No Country for Old Men* Llewelyn Moss, out hunting in west Texas in the 1960's, happens upon some 2 million in cash. He just wants to make a better life for himself and his wife. The money belongs to drug lords so he feels no guilt about keeping it. But those who own that money hire the frightening killer Chigurh to recover the money and kill Llewelyn.

Realizing that Llewelyn is being pursued by an appallingly evil force, Sheriff Bell goes after Llewelyn hoping to extend an opportunity for grace. Approaching retirement, Bell can not wrap his head around the escalating violence and moral decline as he considers his own mortality.

Carson Wells is also sent by the drug lords to retrieve the money. Trying to reason with Llewelyn, he offers to let Llewelyn keep a percentage of the money. Llewelyn, believing that he can sidestep the consequences, rejects both offers in favor of trying to keep the money. Chigurh acts almost like a grim reaper, or fate set in motion by Llewelyn's greed.

While evidence that bad choices have bad results is all around us, we often believe we will be able to avoid them. The spiritual consequences of our decisions are usually even more obscured when we are focused on getting what we want. Stories like *No Country for Old Men* and *Millions* help make the consequences and influences of the good and evil around us more tangible.

Millions is another story of finding a large sum of ill-gotten cash. Money literally falls from the sky into the hands of young brothers Anthony and Damian. Britain is in the process of adopting the Euro, so the fortune, which is in British Pounds, must be spent quickly before the country converts to Euros.

Older brother Anthony immediately begins spending the money while Damian, believing it has been sent by God, seeks spiritual direction for how to use it. The money becomes a burden as Anthony constantly worries about how to hide it, what to buy with it, and whether it will run out. If we interpret lack of resources as lack of self-worth we will never feel good about ourselves and what we do have.

When their father learns about the cash he initially wants to return the money, until the family's home is robbed. Justified by the excuse that they "deserve it," their father and his girlfriend go on a spending frenzy. Meanwhile Damian is quietly giving the money away to the poor.

Anthony and his father see Damian's charity and spirituality as a reaction to his mother's death. But Damian's

Greed

attitude is really rooted in a childlike faith and unselfishness that Anthony and their father cannot fully grasp. Perhaps this sort of spiritual reality is what Jesus meant in Matthew 18 when he talked about coming to him as a little child.

Sometimes people who practice unselfishness and charity can seem naïve. We know that when we give that homeless guy on the corner a dollar he probably is not going to spend it at the grocery store. When we make a donation we expect a tax write-off and perhaps our names on a plaque. Giving has the potential to be joyful and fulfilling if we can overcome cynicism and find a little faith. Damian is an example of someone who sees need and gives with unclenched fists and selfless abandon.

Most of us struggle with the need to feel financially secure. Some of us just love to shop or travel and see money as a means of fulfilling our hopes and dreams. The desire to practice legitimate stewardship can turn us into compulsive misers when the need to save for that unexpected car repair or catastrophic illness is driven by fear.

Materialism

Who can forget Marilyn Monroe singing *Diamonds are a Girl's Best Friend* in *Gentlemen Prefer Blondes*? Not only is there is a certain status connected with owning a diamond, but diamonds are advertised as a material representation of love. This makes diamonds an emotional commodity in our culture.

Corporate, political, and personal greed come together in *Blood Diamond*. Set in Sierra Leone in the 1990's, the film focuses on two greed-based practices. "Freedom fighters" are power-hungry gangs who come into villages and kidnap young boys to brainwash and turn them into "soldiers" in their revolution. They also enslave people to work in diamond mines. These "blood" or "conflict" diamonds are not supposed to enter the world market, but when money is involved there is usually a way around regulations.

Blood Diamond tells the story of Danny, a diamond smuggler, Maddy, a reporter who is in Africa to expose the diamond trade, Solomon, a father who has been taken as a slave to mine diamonds, and Solomon's son Via, who has been taken to train as a soldier. Danny's philosophy is based entirely on taking care of himself at the expense of others. He is a greedy man in business with greedy people.

Solomon's sole concern is for his family. He wants to use a diamond he has taken to buy his son out of military slavery and help his family and village. Maddy believes "people back home wouldn't buy a ring if they knew it had cost someone his hand." The diamond merchants are banking on the opposite.

Like Pontius Pilate washing his hands, the merchants remain deliberately ignorant of the practices that bring the diamonds into their hands. They spin information that might bring these practices to light. They hope that a materialistic public would rather buy diamonds in ignorance instead of questioning the sources of the diamonds in jewelry stores, and perhaps paying more for fair trade items. The movie portrays the incredible violence and heartbreak generated by the collective greed of everyone involved with these diamonds.

Danny begins to question his greedy lifestyle when he meets the passionate Maddy and sees the devastating effect these practices have on Solomon's life. Like the Grinch, Danny's heart begins to expand. Danny must decide whether he can do business as usual considering what

Greed

he now knows. This is not just an adventure movie or a political statement, but a redemption story about one man confronting his own greed.

Some people would rather engage in "serial seeking" rather than actually addressing their issues. In *I Heart Huckabees*, superficial, materialistic characters Brad and Dawn search for meaning. Albert and Tommy, who have already abandoned materialism, fail to find personal fulfillment in anti-materialistic philosophies. For each the search for meaning fails to embrace others.

Huckabees' existential detectives send up pop psychology as characters abandon one philosophical position after another in their desire to find a universe at which each can be the center. *I Heart Huckabees* makes the point that materialism is only one of many ways we can be self-absorbed.

In *Fight Club* Jack ponders "What kind of dining set defines me as a person?" as he grapples with a growing realization that he's been buying furniture to fill an empty space that has nothing to do with his home. Tyler Durden tells Jack that "The things you own end up owning you… advertising has us chasing cars and clothes, working jobs we hate so we can buy shit we don't need." Much of the narrator's mental instability comes because he is struggling with the futility of materialism, yet he lives in a society that ultimately buys into it… and buys and buys and buys.

At no time of year does this consumerism become more prevalent than at Christmas. Ebenezer Scrooge's bitterness and greed keeps him from wanting to participate in the generosity and gift-giving associated with Christmas. On the other end of the spectrum, giving and receiving gifts has launched a multi-million dollar boost for retail sellers of consumer goods. Each year certain items become the "must haves" of the season.

Receiving a certain gift should not boost the social status of a child, but consumerism at Christmas tells a different tale. Bidding on E-bay boosts the price of scarce items well above the recommended retail sales price. Regardless of what advertisers would have us believe, giving a particular item at Christmas is not proof of parental love or success.

What we value is going to translate into what we try to get and keep. Jesus warns us to "Beware, and be on your guard against every form of greed; for not even when one has an abundance does his life consist of his possessions" (Luke 12:15 NAS). How important is our stuff and how much stuff is enough?

Generosity

Sharing is a concept that most of us are taught as children. Some of us do it more out of a sense of obligation than true generosity of spirit. Perhaps when confronted with Mother Teresa or Bono or soup kitchen servants we really wish we felt like being generous instead of feeling guilted into it.

In *It's a Wonderful Life* Mr. Potter sees money as the ultimate end, while George Bailey sees money as a means of building community and helping individuals. Both men work in banking, yet George Bailey has discovered that his work helps those around him while Mr. Potter's work only serves his own interests and those of a small circle of bank stockholders. George's compassion for the needs of others improves the quality of life for an entire town.

Sometimes George's decisions for the benefit of other people cost him personally. When George is in trouble his friends and neighbors line up to help, confirming the adage that "what goes around comes around." This idea is

Greed

understood in many cultures and religions. Some call it karma. Luke records Jesus' words on the subject: "Give, and you will receive. Your gift will return to you in full - pressed down, shaken together to make room for more, running over, and poured into your lap. The amount you give will determine the amount you get back" (Luke 6:38).

Pay it Forward presents another picture of generous living. In response to a school assignment about changing the world young Trevor decides that paying it forward can cause positive change. His idea is to do something life-changing for three people and they in turn "pay it forward" to three more people, increasing the help exponentially. His experiment inspires people all over the country to behave unselfishly and, in doing so, to discover that each has something to give others. If need is a problem and greed is a problem then generosity is a solution for both.

In *Babette's Feast*, as a refugee from another country Babette has lived on the generosity of strangers. Babette has been exposed to cultural experiences outside the small-town sphere of her new friends. She and her hosts never completely overcome some of the awkward differences between them. When Babette wins the lottery, rather than using her winnings to buy herself a more comfortable lifestyle, she uses her resources to create something special for the people who have helped her.

Babette gives lavishly, demonstrating Paul's idea of preferring one another in brotherly love (Rom. 12:10b). She uses all her money on a one-night party for her friends with the seemingly wasteful passion of the woman who pours out expensive perfume to wash the feet of Christ. The way that she gives everything she has to give her friends an experience that they cannot provide for themselves echoes Christ's gift of salvation.

Sinema7

Treasure

An honest assessment of our emotional attachment to our things might reveal what we really treasure. Captain Barbossa, one of the pirates in *Pirates of the Caribbean*, warns that the more they squandered their treasure and their lives "the more we came to realize the drink would not satisfy, food turned to ash in our mouths, and all the pleasurable company in the world could not slake our lust…. Compelled by greed, we were, but now we are consumed by it."

Besides money we can treasure our time, our labor, and our material possessions. "If you think of life as like a big pie, you can try to hold the whole pie and kill yourself trying to keep it, or you can slice it up and give some to the people around you, and you still have plenty left for yourself" comments Jay Leno. That may seem to be an easy comment for someone who has lots of resources, but sometimes those of us with limited resources are the most protective of them.

So often fear keeps us from behaving generously. God wants our trust, even when it's not immediately evident how our needs will be met. There is a tendency to try to keep everything we have just in case it runs out. Paul presents another approach: "And God will generously provide all you need. Then you will always have everything you need and plenty left over to share with others" (2 Cor. 9:8). When we see what we have, however much or little that may be, as resources to be used rather than treasure to be hoarded we can develop generous attitudes.

Jesus presents a bold antidote to greed: "Sell your possessions and give to those in need. This will store up treasure for you in heaven! And the purses of heaven never get old or develop holes. Your treasure will be safe; no thief can steal it and no moth can destroy it" (Luke 12:33). Sometimes we have to let go of those things we've made too important in order change our focus. God wants to be our source of provision and the focus of our attention.

What we devote our time and effort acquiring is an indication of what we believe is important. Jesus said that "Wherever your treasure is, there the desires of your heart will also be" (Matt. 6:21). Greed is an indication that our devotion is focused on money and possessions. Paul pulled no punches, telling the Colossians "Don't be greedy, for a greedy person is an idolater, worshiping the things of this world" (Col. 3:5). It may not seem like we are worshipping our stuff, but if we derive status, security, and hope from our stuff then we are allowing money and possessions to do for us what God wants to do for us. God wants to be our treasure, and also wants us to treasure what He treasures, which is people, not stuff.

7 SLOTH

Uh, I don't do much really, I just read, and work here, and, uh, sleep and eat, and, uh, watch movies - Anti-Artist, *Slacker*

It's not that I'm lazy; it's that I just don't care - Peter Gibbons, *Office Space*

I'm not lazy, I just... Lisa, finish my sentence for me! - Bart Simpson, *Monty Can't Buy Me Love* episode of *The Simpsons*

I'm too lazy to hold a grudge - Sid the Sloth, *Ice Age*

People who throw kisses are mighty hopelessly lazy - Bob Hope

Sometimes he would accuse chestnuts of being lazy. A sort of general malaise that only the genius possess and the insane lament - Dr. Evil, *Austin Powers: International Man of Mystery*

Last week I helped my friend stay put. It's a lot easier than helping someone move - Mitch Hedberg, stand-up comic

Sloth

"Leave me where I am I'm only sleeping…" This line from the Beatles' song *I'm Only Sleeping* describes the attitude of the slothful. Nothing seems to evoke passion. Nothing seems worth the effort. Dorothy Sayers describes sloth as "the sin which believes in nothing, cares for nothing, enjoys nothing, loves nothing, hates nothing, finds purpose in nothing, lives for nothing, and only remains alive because there is nothing it would die for."

Sometimes we just don't want to deal. We retreat or procrastinate. Our problems may make us sleepy or send us to the movies. When we take on personal and professional projects, minimizing inconvenience and avoiding trouble is often a deciding factor. In relationships, avoiding confrontation becomes more important than communicating. Sometimes sloth comes from apathy, and sometimes it comes from fear and insecurity. Sometimes it's just about comfort and convenience.

Negativity figures into sloth. Doubt, defeat, and disillusionment can be paralyzing. We may doubt our abilities, doubt that the outcome will be successful, or doubt that we are doing anything significant. With so little motivation, putting forth effort seems like a waste of time.

Avoidance

In *Failure to Launch* 35-year-old Tripp still lives at home with his parents. After a traumatic event his life is stuck in neutral. His parents think it's time for him to move on but continue to enable him. What may have started as a supportive gesture on their part and real need on Tripp's part has become a comfortable, unchallenging existence for Tripp. A guy still living in his parents house is a deal-breaker for most women, so he sees living there as a way to avoid any real emotional involvement. He fears another loss. Tripp is putting off independence as long as he can get by with it. Fearing he will never take the initiative to move out, his parents resort to drastic measures.

Committing to a course of action eliminates all the other possibilities. For many people closing off options can almost feel like a trap. What if a better choice presents itself later? What if what's next is not as enjoyable as what's now? What if this is the wrong decision? These thoughts can make us drag our feet. Eventually this sort of procrastination becomes a habit. "Someday" becomes our timeline for everything.

Camp Nowhere is a fake summer camp created by a resourceful group of kids who want to avoid the work and commitment involved in attending one of those very purposeful "improvement" camps their parents have selected. They blackmail a former drama teacher, Dennis Van Welker, to act as a fake counselor and cover for them to their parents and other adults. Dennis is a burned out hippie who can't seem to hold a challenging job, but he does remember why he got into teaching in the first place. He describes a purposeful decision with the goal to help and inspire kids. As problems arise in his life he runs away to avoid facing the consequences, leaving his dreams behind.

Some of the kids are being pushed to excel by ambitious parents, while others are dumped in camp because they are inconvenient. Though they are unwilling to cooperate with their parents' ideas about personal improvement, left to their own devices the kids engage and begin developing their personal gifts and talents, along with the usual camp shenanigans. Dennis and the kids are pushed into taking responsibility, and Dennis rediscovers some of the passion he's lost along the way.

A few chapters after writing off all work as "meaningless" the writer of Ecclesiastes finds that embracing the joys of life is the way to go: "So go ahead. Eat your food with joy, and drink your wine with a happy heart, for God approves of this! Wear fine clothes, with a splash of cologne! Live happily with the woman you love through all the meaningless days of life that God has given you under the sun. Whatever you do, do well" (Ecc. 9:7-8).

Neither Tripp nor Dennis is living the lives they expected. Their lives don't look like other people think they ought to look either. Nobody likes to feel like a disappointment. It may seem better that people think we don't care than to have them think we are incompetent. We can tell ourselves, and others, what a great job we would do if we actually cared. It can look like we don't care when we actually care too much.

Hopelessness

Then there are those of us who actually don't care. Rather than "sloth," 4th century writer Evagrius used the Latin word "acedia," which literally means "absence of caring." Acedia can lead to boredom, cynicism, and just plain exhaustion. Constant boredom or cynicism reflects a lack of hope. A life that consists of just going through the motions lacks hope.

M. Night Shyamalan addresses lack of hope and finding purpose in several of his movies. Cleveland Heep, in *Lady in the Water*, is in a holding pattern in his life. He's suffered loss that has him stuck in depression and unable to find hope for the future. Cleveland has simply settled for mediocrity and chosen the path of least resistance. A situation that

Sloth

demands heroic action leads him toward freedom and hope.

In this fantasy, Story, who is from another world, can only be returned through the cooperation of a number of people who fulfill particular roles. Cleveland takes responsibility for identifying these people and getting them involved in the task of rescuing Story. He brings a group of people into community and reveals the unique value and unexpected strengths in each one, including Cleveland himself. As he commits to meeting someone else's need Cleveland is able to let go of his debilitating grief.

"Acedia" is still used today as a medical term, defined as "A mental syndrome, the chief features of which are listlessness, carelessness, apathy, and melancholia." Thomas Aquinas spoke to a lack of hope when he explained that even though acedia might be "sorrow which is about a real evil, [it] is evil in its effect, if it so oppresses man as to draw him away entirely from good deeds." Though real evil affects our lives and the lives of those we love, if we begin to feel overwhelmed by these legitimately bad circumstances we may become so resigned that we give up.

Dante categorized sloth as "insufficient love," while he grouped lust, gluttony, and greed as "excessive love" and wrath, envy, and pride as "misdirected love." Sometimes this insufficient love reflects an unwillingness to place anyone or anything above our own comfort. In other cases it may reflect an insufficient love of self.

In *Ferris Bueller's Day Off* three friends skip school to have a day of fun in Chicago. Ferris is optimistic and completely secure in his parents' love. He believes in himself and in his own ability to influence the world around him. Ferris' neurotic friend Cameron worries about everything. He believes that he is not a priority to his father. Cameron feels insecure, inadequate, and powerless. This makes it seem pointless to get out there and live life.

Cameron doesn't do anything unless Ferris pushes him. He doesn't want to commit himself or have to defend his decisions, so he lets others make decisions for him. In one scene he is so conflicted he gets in and out of the car several times, trying to decide whether or not to skip school with Ferris.

Cameron lets Ferris set the plan, then worries the whole time about the decisions. He lets Ferris decide. He lets his father decide. Cameron doesn't feel he actually has a say in what happens to him.

In one scene Cameron stands in an art gallery and experiences a crisis moment. As he stares at the Seurat painting "Sunday Afternoon on La Grande Jatte" and focuses in on a figure in the center of the picture he realizes that she has no distinguishable features on her face. His sense of hopelessness and worthlessness comes crashing down on him as he confronts his own lack of personal identity. His father is important. Ferris is important. He's just Cameron.

Meanwhile Ferris joins a parade and sings from a float, making a dedication "To a young man who doesn't think he's seen anything good today — Cameron Frye, this one's for you." Cameron and Ferris are having the same day, but experiencing it differently. Ferris engages the people around him and delights in everything he experiences; Cameron can only see his own misery. Cameron can't let himself enjoy the day the way Ferris does. Ultimately Cameron Frye's day off is about seeing his state of paralysis, and working up the courage to break out of it.

Fear can paralyze. We may fear failure to the point that we expect to fail. We can learn to trust ourselves to be successful, to trust others to love us if we happen to fail, and to trust God to bless our efforts with success (his version, not ours).

Boredom

In *Hitchhiker's Guide to the Galaxy* Marvin the Robot has a brain the "size of a planet." His role as "your plastic pal who's fun to be with" leaves him bored with nothing challenging to accomplish or discover. He is in a cycle in which hopelessness leads to cynicism and cynicism leads to boredom, which leads to depression, which leads to hopelessness. Marvin is trapped in a world with no flow.

Psychologist Mihaly Csikszentmihalyi defines flow as "being completely involved in an activity for its own sake. The ego falls away. Time flies. Every action, movement, and thought follows inevitably from the previous one, like playing jazz. Your whole being is involved, and you're using your skills to the utmost." Csikszentmihalyi believes that flow happens when our skills match the circumstances we must face, and when we are acting with clear goals.

Some of us, like Marvin, possess underutilized skills, gifts, and talents. We may have boring jobs that do not challenge us. Feeling this way all the time is a strong indication that it's time to evaluate both attitude and occupational choices. However, we cannot expect to experience flow all the time. Sometimes life involves tedium. We are likely to experience less boredom if we approach boring tasks with good humor, imagination, and grace.

Laziness

Some of us just don't like to work. We want to have fun. We want our needs met with as little effort as possible.

We absolutely are willing to settle for less. As the reputation for laziness grows it becomes something that defines who we are. Giving it up would mean redefining ourselves.

Billy Madison never wants to grow up, and until he faces the threat of losing everything he hasn't worked for he's content with irresponsibility as a lifestyle. Billy likes drinking, sex, parties, and lying around on his father's estate with his lazy friends. In order to prove to his father that he is worthy of the family business he must go back to school and pass every grade. As he moves through each grade in school he develops a greater sense of responsibility. The young friends he makes in each grade help him to gain greater compassion for other people. Billy never transforms into an overachiever, but he does develop a willingness to embrace adulthood and responsibility.

We all need a little silliness, but many of us seek entertainment as an end goal. We find outlets for this everywhere in our culture. Many of us would rather get our news from *The Daily Show* and *The Colbert Report*. If we have to learn something we'd prefer edutainment over lecture. We watch *The Food Network* instead of actually cooking something. We carry around devices that allow us to listen to music and play games until life interrupts us. There is so much to care about that life can be overwhelming.

Perhaps this trend toward constant entertainment is an attempt to escape. Most issues cannot be reduced to sound bites, or resolved in a few minutes worth of dialogue. Life is complicated and may require effort on our part to process and action on our part to solve. We may have to act on things that we are still conflicted about and may not be able to resolve.

In the movie *The Big Lebowski* The Dude is identified as "the laziest man in Los Angeles County" while his

Sloth

opposite, the Big Lebowski, is successful, rich, industrious, and supremely unhappy. The Dude seems to be very satisfied with his unmaterialistic lifestyle yet seems to really need something to anchor his life, like his rug.

At the insistence of his friend Walter he becomes involved in a complicated intrigue involving his stolen rug, a case of mistaken identify, millions of dollars, and a woman's life. As the plot thickens and the tension escalates The Dude's focus remains, "I just want my rug back." His rug seems to tie his life together as much as it "ties the room together."

Walter and The Dude are both apathetic about the present and disinterested in the future. Throughout the movie both characters continuously refer to the past. The Dude is a former hippie protester, and Walter is a Vietnam vet. Each seems to have found his identity in a stereotype from the 70's.

The Big Lebowski is materialistic and narrow minded. The materialism of his generation offers nothing to inspire the Dude, who has rejected materialism. The women in the movie represent the self-absorbed attitude of a generation that has concluded that nothing matters. This nihilistic attitude also bothers The Dude.

Since no generation has legitimate answers he clings to the 70's when, as one of the Seattle Seven, he at least tried to make things better. Currently the bowling alley is the one place where the Dude feels purposeful. His unwillingness to sell out or compromise actually indicates a greater sense of purpose than his lifestyle would indicate.

The Dude seems to have figured out what he doesn't believe. He rejects both nihilism and materialism. Lack of meaning and purpose has led The Dude to adopt an attitude similar to that of the writer of Ecclesiastes, who says "People leave this world no better off than when they came. All their hard work is for nothing - like working for the wind" (5:16b). Rather than working for the wind, "The Dude abides" on whatever fulfillment White Russians, a soak in the tub, and bowling can give him until he figures out what else matters.

Finding passion

Sloth attaches itself to our spiritual DNA. It becomes an aspect of our personalities rather than just an occasional action, or in this case, inaction. "I know I'm lazy but someday I'll deal with it…" or, "I have every reason to feel like this and I deserve to kick back for awhile…" Sloth may become so ingrained in how we see ourselves and how others see us that we embrace it as part of our identity.

In the movie *Office Space* Peter Gibbons dreams of "doing nothing." He tells "the Bobs" (the efficiency experts) that his only motivation is to avoid having a parade of bosses telling him what he did wrong. "Where's the motivation in that, Bob?" he asks. This movie shows how labor without passion can wound a soul.

Solomon said "Where there is no vision the people perish" (Prov. 29:18 KJV). Without vision and passion we tend to take the path of least resistance, seeking immediate gratification and comfort. The opposing cardinal virtue to sloth is diligence, or zeal. Zeal is the energetic response of the heart to God's commands. Love, joy, and self-control seem to be necessary components to zeal; and hope is central.

There is joy in doing what we love. Self-control and discipline are what help us do it well. We may be able to fulfill our obligations without a true sense of purpose, but this sort of diligence is a prison without passion. In the movie *Chariots of Fire* Eric Liddell tells his sister that "when I run I feel God's pleasure." He takes a gift, something he loves to do, something he has the natural ability to do, and develops it to the degree that he becomes an Olympic Champion. We each have been gifted with abilities and traits that are there both to give pleasure and service. We can do what we love, and inspire and help others to experience God's pleasure. Each of us needs to find God's unique purpose for our lives, embrace that, and focus our energies outward.

Living purposefully

Hope and trust come back into play here. We need to believe that what we do matters. We hope that what we do will have a positive impact on our own lives and on the lives of others. At its worst, sloth leads to spiritual withdrawal. We may use sarcasm, negativity, and passive-aggression to cope with pain and disappointment. Developing a habit of inaction can lead to actual loss of energy and creativity over time. Hope leads us to really engage.

In *August Rush* Evan dreams a big, audacious dream. He believes that an unlikely miracle will happen if he attains his dream. He can only work toward his purpose and trust that everything that is out of his control will fall into place. This movie is not just about a young boy's talent, but about his hopefulness. Evan makes himself utterly vulnerable, experiences disappointment and betrayal, yet remains hopeful. Evan is a picture of the genuine, unpretentious, authentic people who Jesus was talking about when he said "blessed are the pure in heart" in his Sermon on the Mount (Matt. 5-7). Paul wrote that "God causes everything to work together for the good of those who love God and are called according to his purpose for them" (Rom. 8:28). The choices of all the characters are marked by the hand of God responding to Evan's faith.

As individuals we are all gifted with talents and have unique interests that are meant to benefit others as well as ourselves. Additionally, all Christians are challenged with two important purposes. First, The Great Commandment is to love God with our whole hearts, minds, and souls, and to love our neighbors as ourselves (Luke 10:27). Second, The Great Commission is to tell others about His love and redemption (Matt. 28:19-20). When we focus on others rather than self there is no guarantee of personal comfort or convenience. There is, however, great potential for fulfillment and belonging. We must weigh whether opening ourselves up to the discomfort that is bound to come with hope and purpose is worth the satisfaction that accompanies it.

Goethe said "Hell begins the day God grants you the vision to see all you could have done, should have done, and would have done, but did not do." Most of our regrets are about things we failed to do, not about things we tried to do but failed. When we embrace zeal over sloth we may find we can commit ourselves more fully.

Living enthusiastically

In *Uncle Buck* a school principal tells Buck that his niece is a "silly-heart and a dreamer" who doesn't "take her school career seriously." He responds that he "doesn't want to know a six-year-old is isn't a silly-heart and a dreamer." I personally prefer sixty-year-olds who haven't forgotten how to be silly-hearts and dreamers as well. There is a difference between childishness and being childlike. Billy Madison is childish and has to learn to accept responsibility. August Rush's sense of wonder and willingness to believe in miracles embodies childlike faith.

Sloth

The French have an expression, "joie de vivre," which means joy of life. It means joy in everything, a comprehensive joy, a philosophy of life that involves the whole being. Both Ferris Bueller and August Rush demonstrate this.

Enthusiasm is not a discipline. We can't talk ourselves into it or work ourselves into it. What we can do is jump in and keep our eyes open. As we shift focus from ourselves to the purpose at hand we may eventually find our flow, or at least fleeting glimpses of it. We may just find that we can give our whole being and whole effort to what we are doing, and experience joy while we are doing it. This joy is not something we can manufacture, but rather something that God brings about when we let him disentangle the sloth that wraps itself around our souls.

According to the writer of Hebrews, "Faith is the confidence that what we hope for will actually happen; it gives us assurance about things we cannot see" (Heb. 11:1). Slothfulness obscures the vision. We may believe that God is really in control but we don't actually trust Him to lead us. We may believe that God has our best interests at heart but we can't take our focus off the problem or the pain. Without trust and hope as motivators change is too hard, too much work, too painful, too uncertain. The heart of the gospel is God's gift of real change. Just as the cross changes our status with God from guilty to forgiven, every aspect of our lives - spiritual, mental, emotional, physical, relational, and circumstantial is meant to undergo change that reconciles us to God, and gives us hope and joy.

7 ANGER

Fear is the path to the Dark Side. Fear leads to anger, anger leads to hate, hate leads to suffering - Yoda, *Star Wars: The Empire Strikes Back*

I'm mad as hell and I'm not going to take it anymore! - Howard Beale, *Network*

See, when you make a move out of frustration or anger, it always ends in catastrophe - John Casey, *Bobby*

You know something princess; you are ugly when you're angry - Lonestar, *Spaceballs*

Don't drive angry! Don't drive angry! - Phil Connors, *Groundhog Day*

Don't you think there's a lot of uh, a lot of anger floating around this island… A lot of angst. A lot of I'm sixteen I'm angry at my father syndrome? I mean, grow up! - Stanley Goodspeed, *The Rock*

Last year, it was Saturday Night Specials… now it's heavy stuff. People must be getting madder about something - Ruth, *48 Hours*

Anger

Throughout the Middle Ages, when the seven deadly sins were listed "anger" was called "wrath." As opposed to the occasional episode of anger that is a reaction to a specific event, wrath is a general disposition of frustration, aggression, revenge, malice, or bitterness. Anger can become a habit because it gives us a sense of power.

In *Se7en* serial killer John Doe chooses victims he believes are guilty of the seven deadly sins and murders each in a method that reflects that sin. He plots out an elaborately twisted morality play for the two sins he saves for last.

The person he considers "Wrath" comes across as brash and impatient, rather than downright angry. Throughout the movie John Doe sets up this character to explode. As if on cue this character does become angrier and less willing to think objectively. When Doe can count on "Wrath" to play his role, Doe commits his final murder, one which might have been prevented had "Wrath" been able to control his disposition. The question remains whether Doe causes this character to become wrath or whether he is wrath all along.

Frustration

Feeling helpless can lead to frustration. Even the impotent anger of frustration can make us feel more powerful. Often those of us who anger easily have a low tolerance for frustration. We can't take inconveniences or annoyances in stride. If we feel threatened, insulted, or unjustly treated we want to lash out.

Fits of rage can be frightening to onlookers, but we may not even recognize that we are overreacting. Little deals become big deals, and outbursts over small things look ridiculous to those around us. Emotion takes over and we stop responding logically or compassionately. Anger becomes a habit. Our response to the world is to take offense. Over time we move from experiencing angry episodes to becoming angry people.

We may feel the need to vent. Some people scream, hit things, honk the horn, or curse. At one time psychologists believed that fits of rage could provide an immediate gratification or release, called catharsis. Psychological and health researchers now believe that catharsis actually prolongs the episode of rage and probably has negative health effects.

While being honest about anger is good, venting hostility escalates the situation rather than resolving it. In *Star Wars* Luke Skywalker is challenged by Obi-Wan Kenobi and Yoda to fight evil without hate and anger. This inability to control rage is the beginning of Anakin Skywalker's descent into his Darth Vader persona.

In *The House of Sand and Fog* Kathy is wrongfully evicted from her home. She is frustrated in her attempts to resolve the issue with local government officials. When we feel wronged we tend to want to understand why, and assigning blame seems to help in that process. We may feel less powerless when we have somewhere to direct our anger.

Kathy turns her anger on both Behrani, the man who buys her house, and on the government bureaucrats who accidentally displace her. The situation is too complicated for a true villain to emerge, yet both Kathy and Behrani want to make sense of their problems and make one another scapegoats. Understanding that no one is to blame comes too late to prevent the tragedy that their initial anger has set in motion.

Occasional venting becomes habitual. When anger comes to a head a single event can trigger an emotional snap. In *Falling Down* Bill's layoff leads to a series of confrontations over minor annoyances. After abandoning his car because he's become too impatient to wait in snarled traffic, Bill begins walking home across L.A. Throughout the movie he engages in verbal and physical abuse of people who happen to be involved in the minor annoyances we might encounter on an ordinary day.

When he is told he is two minutes late to order from the breakfast menu he launches into a cathartic rant at the people behind the counter in a hamburger restaurant over, of all things, their name tags. "Why am I calling you by your first names? I don't even know you. I still call my boss "Mister," and I've been working for him for seven years, but all of a sudden I walk in here and I'm calling you Rick and Sheila like we're in some kind of AA meeting... I don't want to be your buddy, Rick. I just want some breakfast." Perhaps it started from the pressure of losing his job, but with each encounter his level of aggression escalates. Every act of aggression makes the next one more natural for him.

Aggression

In *Lord of the Rings* Sauron forges the ring of power, "And into this ring he poured his cruelty, his malice, and his will to dominate all life." We may not be out to dominate all life but some of us would settle for the highway, the office, or the classroom. Rage has become an increasing problem in our society. From road rage to school shootings, people are expressing their anger and desire to dominate through aggression.

In the movie *Fight Club* Tyler Durden describes his

aggression like this: "We're the middle children of history, man. No purpose or place. We have no Great War. No Great Depression. Our Great War's a spiritual war... our Great Depression is our lives. We've all been raised on television to believe that one day we'd all be millionaires and movie gods, and rock stars. But we won't. And we're slowly learning that fact. And we're very, very pissed off."

The characters in *Fight Club* engage in violence as a means of self-affirmation. This film explores the idea that men in western society often feel that they are emasculated. There seems to be no room for the average man's more aggressive characteristics in a society based on consumerism, corporate position, and political power. Physical aggression may be acceptable as entertainment but there is no place for it in boardrooms and malls. Aggression must be diverted into more subtle channels.

It is this subtle but constant agitation that causes the unnamed narrator to turn to Tyler Durden to find some sort of outlet for the aggression that he is socially restrained from expressing. The men in *Fight Club* find satisfaction and connection in this very direct form of communication. We may not seek *Fight Club*'s extreme channel for aggression, but we may be able to identify with the isolation and frustration that inspires it.

Fear, sadness, loneliness, even kindness seem weak. Anger is a means of engaging with other people without feeling exposed. Aggressive people need to feel they have control and dominance.

Malice

In *Mean Girls* school is described as a "shark tank." There is definitely a pecking order within the various social circles.

The top girls, the "Plastics," are led by Regina George who defines what is acceptable, what is stylish, and what is "cool." She determines who is "in" and who is "out." The threat of losing friends, being outcast from the group, or losing status with peers is used by these mean girls to control others and to feel secure themselves.

According to author Rosalind Wiseman, whose book *Mean Girls* inspired the movie, "Often it's girls with high self-esteem" (who do this). Psychologists call it "relational aggression" when someone inflicts personal and social pain on others for sport, or to gain social advantage. Having friends should mean supportive relationships, but instead becomes a quest for social status. While everyone recognizes that the Plastics are manipulative and malicious, they also accept their power as a matter of course. One of their victims, Janis Ian, challenges their power, but it is not until newcomer Cady calls them on their meanness that they are really exposed.

Bullying and back biting not only takes place on school yards and in high school hallways but in workplaces as well. People will put up with a lot of maliciousness when their ability to earn a living is at stake. The movies have given us many "bosses from hell." Sometimes malice is expressed in something as subtle as how work space is assigned. Who can forget Lumbergh banishing Milton to the basement in *Office Space*?

Some bosses may withhold credit that could lead to professional status, like *Working Girl*'s Katherine Parker, who steals an idea from secretary Tess Mcgill and touts it as her own. Then there is Franklin Hart in *9 to 5*, who belittles and sexually harasses his female employees, secure in knowing he has power over their paychecks. In *Glengarry Glen Ross* Blake's motivational style is to fire everyone, tell them what failures they are, and then give them a week to earn back their jobs. When anger is expressed from the top down the results can be ugly, and the victims may feel they have little recourse.

Resentment

For some of us confrontations take so much emotional energy that we just pick. Our stockpiled resentments may be expressed as gossip, demeaning comments, or through sly humor, like Jim's funny comments and pranks in the television series *The Office*. In early seasons Jim insists the job is just an extended stop on his career path, stating "If this were my career I'd have to throw myself in front of a train." He's really a nice guy but instead of embracing his present situation he makes sly comments and performs funny pranks to relieve his boredom. His attitude tempers a bit when he later becomes a boss himself. Other passive-aggressive methods might be the silent treatment or playing the victim. Most of us who engage in passive-aggressive behavior feel that we will lose in a direct confrontation, but still want to send a message that we're really, really mad.

Resentment also builds when we feel that we've sacrificed and now we're owed. The sense of obligation we feel toward loved ones may sometimes cause us to feel resentment. Mothers are particularly good at projecting this particular brand of anger. Guilt and resentment in marriages may build when couples feel one another is taking the relationship for granted, or taking advantage of the comfort level that marriage provides. We may end up feeling trapped in our most intimate relationship.

For Lloyd and Caroline Chausseur in *The Ref*, bickering has become a way of life. The title character, Gus, kidnaps the Chausseurs after a bungled burglary but finds he has to play referee to this dysfunctional family. He describes the experience as "the fifth ring of hell."

Caroline is bitter because her life hasn't met her expectations. Lloyd hasn't met them either. She uses her disappointment to justify an affair, and constantly rehashes the events that led up to their current, unsatisfactory circumstances. Caroline has developed a victim mentality in which she believes she has every right to complain, and has no power to change the circumstances of her life. Waaah, waaah, waaah….

Lloyd also feels trapped and has shut down communication with Caroline. He points out that Caroline leaves "the deciding" to him, then complains about the decisions. Lloyd expresses his resentment: "You… think you have some right to life working out the way you want it to, and when it doesn't, you get to act the way you want. The only trouble with that is someone has to be responsible… You think every morning I wake up, look in the mirror and say 'Gee I'm glad I'm me'…" Lloyd has built a wall of bitterness to protect himself. No hope means no disappointment.

Lloyd and Caroline's passive-aggressive bickering is their primary form of interaction. Only when Gus ties them together do they really begin to talk. Being trapped together helps them to communicate how each has felt trapped separately. While they have no problem expressing their anger, they avoid addressing the big issues in their lives that might require change.

It can be scary, but sometimes we need to confront, even if we lose. We can and should hone our communication skills, gather good data, and build consensus - all the things we are supposed to do in order to bring about change. The Apostle Paul advised the Ephesians not to "sin by letting anger control you. Don't let the sun go down while you are still angry, for anger gives a foothold to the devil" (Eph. 4:26-27). Harboring bitterness inflames anger. We can't control every circumstance. We can't control other people. What we can control is how we react initially, and what sort of baggage we choose to carry.

Revenge

Payback is said to be sweet. "Don't get mad, get even" has been a Kennedy family motto, an Aerosmith song lyric, a bumper sticker, and an unofficial presidential campaign slogan. Road rage, acts of retaliations like honking the horn, flipping someone off, or deliberately boxing someone in are seen as payback for a perceived or real discourtesy. It's sort of satisfying to see those who have hurt others suffer. While these behaviors may seem sort of petty and humorous, in some cases revenge has changed the course of history.

The film *Munich* presents a serious take on vengeance. Avner, a Mossad agent, seeks revenge for the terrorist slayings of eleven Israeli athletes at the 1972 Munich Olympics. He becomes so focused on his mission, justifying great violence, that this "righteous" anger takes its toll on his personality and relationships, as well as on the political and social landscape of Israel itself. In this film anger results in a cycle of violence, mired in thousands of years of anger and resentment that, Avner says, "will never end in peace."

Many of us are just looking for an excuse to be outraged. Rather than being about protection, it becomes about judgment. Vengeance may be the Lord's but many of us would love to help. The compulsion to defend slips into a drive to avenge.

Will Munny in *Unforgiven* struggles with a predisposition for violence. Having left his violent past behind this former gunfighter has moved on to farming, marriage, and children. He stands at his wife's grave and declares himself a changed man.

Will is drawn back in to his former lifestyle when Sheriff Little Bill Daggett ignores a brutal attack on a young prostitute and her outraged madam offers a bounty in order to secure just punishment. The young "Schofield Kid" recruits Will to join him in a bounty hunt. Will needs the money and convinces himself that the cause is worthy. He joins the kid and brings along former outlaw Ned Logan.

While moral outrage is the catalyst that draws the men back into their former lifestyle, each reacts differently to renewed participation in violence and killing. Ned realizes he is no longer the man he once was and tries to back out. With each killing the husband and father Will believes he has become recedes, and the killer he was before emerges. Giving up the lifestyle has not removed aggression from Will's heart.

Paul describes this struggle for change in Romans 7:23 "There is another power within me that is at war with my mind. This power makes me a slave to the sin that is still within me." Rather than recognize the war within, Will concludes that because he is still attracted to violence that he has no hope of redemption. Will believes that he is no more deserving of forgiveness than the bad guys he is hunting.

Like a bounty hunter, a hit man may be the ultimate blend of angry retribution and dispassionate violence. *Pulp Fiction's* Jules embraces his job. He embellishes his work by quoting a fictional Bible verse represented as Ezekiel 25:17, because it is a "cool thing to say" before killing someone.

When another character shoots at him six times at

Anger

point blank range Jules experiences what he describes as this "moment of clarity" in which "God got involved." In contrast his partner Vincent views the same event as coincidence. Jules tries to work out this change of heart as he attempts to talk another character out of killing, using the very "verse" he quotes before killing. He says, "Either you are the evil man and I am the righteous, or you are the weak and I am the tyranny of evil men. But I am trying real hard to be the shepherd." Jules seems to realize that it is possible both to separate his actions from his disposition and for his disposition to change. Jules entertains the concept that God might have some control over real world events, and that an actual possibility for redemption exists.

Patience

We need to feel that we have some control over our lives and ourselves, and anger can sometimes seem to contribute to feelings of control. People we love and trust will disappoint us. We will find ourselves at the mercy of strangers. We sometimes feel threatened and abused. We may be tempted to assign blame. If we think we are being manipulated by forces stronger than ourselves, we may feel that we must either fight or surrender. Patience should never be mistaken for complacency.

Reinhold Niebuhr wrote a prayer in which he said, "Help me accept the things I cannot change, change the things I can, and help me to have the wisdom to know the difference." Acceptance is not surrender; it is finding a place of peace. If we become angry over things we cannot change we waste personal energy that is intended for something more constructive. In acceptance we acknowledge that some things are out of our control, and that some of them are going to be painful. We agree to be honest about our pain rather than masking it with anger.

In *Good Will Hunting* Will has no patience explaining his mathematical thinking to his professor. He has no patience with developing a give and take relationship with his girlfriend. He has an "I just want this over with" attitude. Will would rather be angry than vulnerable. He needs to experience the tension that all these relationships create in order to learn to trust other people, but his reactions are classic "fight" or "flight." He is antagonistic in job interviews. He breaks up with his girlfriend. Will has no patience with the process of working through his emotional baggage.

"It's not your fault" says psychologist Sean Maguire, as Will finally lays down the issues that cause so much anger and alienation in his life. After a series of angry outbursts which land him on probation and loses him the love of his life, Will finally reaches a place in which he can let go of his destructive anger. He accepts the past he cannot change and is ready to participate in decisions about his future that he can control. Release from guilt and anger changes Will's future.

Forgiveness

Bitterness and anger eat away at us. We may even forget the original cause of our bitterness and simply cling to an angry attitude like a security blanket. We find ourselves cycling through this anger even in the small things in life that affect us. If the TV cable box stops working properly, some of the channels may be missing or the picture might be distorted We have to reset it in order to restore full functionality and access to all the channels. Forgiveness acts like a hard reset for anger.

Anger

The sort of forgiveness Christ offers is like a hard reset for our entire lives. Not only are we forgiven, but it is as if no offense ever occurred. Any baggage we carry is entirely on our side of the relationship; he holds no grudge and remembers no failure so that we are "new every morning." God is omniscient, which means he knows everything. The act of forgetting on his part is deliberate and somewhat miraculous. In light of that, carrying around baggage that he doesn't even see seems rather pointless. If we are followers of Christ much of our journey involves letting go of our tendencies toward any of the seven deadly sins. Forgiveness provides freedom and health for our souls.

Is it possible for us to forgive other people as completely as Christ forgave? How would it feel to be forgiven in that way by someone we've hurt? Something heavy lifts when forgiveness happens, regardless of whether or not we can restore a relationship or mend a situation through the act of forgiveness. We find peace when we let go of anger.

Grace in conflict

Sometimes a manipulative leader combined with bad socioeconomic conditions can escalate misdirected anger into a political or social movement, or even war. Sometimes leaders identify a group of people as scapegoats for the problems a nation may experience. *Schindler's List* and *Hotel Rwanda* present a contrast between escalating prejudice, social tension, and individuals who choose to act against the tide of this sort of anger. Oskar Schindler and Paul Rusesabagina both protect people who are threatened and try to maintain normalcy and order in the face of the chaos around them. They take aggressive action and react with kindness toward violent, unjust behavior on the parts of others. Aggressive acts coupled with moral outrage have been at the root of much social change. Within even appropriate expressions of anger, however, there is always the need to examine the heart.

Martin Luther King, Jr. said that "The ultimate measure of a person is not where one stands in moments of comfort and convenience, but where one stands in times of challenge and controversy." And it is not only where one stands, but how one stands there. We can be right on an issue and completely wrong in the way in which we express our convictions. Grace involves taking a stand that will never be undermined by the way we express it. Jesus was a master of this.

When challenged, Jesus often asked searching questions. He wasn't afraid that his ideas were going to be shot down. He wasn't threatened by authority figures or critics. Often getting angry is a way to avoid having a conversation we're afraid of losing. A confident and peaceful attitude helps us to focus on the issue. Many times we assume a disagreement is personal when it is actually ideological. Allowing people to disagree with us in a gracious, friendly way keeps the channels of communication open for future discussion. The goal is to communicate, not to win.

What Jesus said about forgiveness

After teaching the Lord's Prayer, which deals with a lot of different issues, the one line "Forgive us as we forgive those who have hurt us" was what Jesus chose to focus on next. He said that if we do not forgive other people we cannot be forgiven ourselves. He later says something that emphasizes how very powerful forgiveness is. He says that what we forgive on earth is forgiven in heaven. This idea holds powerful implications.

We may have an objective handle on truth. We may be able to theologically defend our religious doctrinal positions, but authentic Christianity is measured, according to Jesus, Paul, and John, by our ability to love and to forgive.

7 ENVY

Don't waste your time on jealously, sometimes you're ahead, sometimes you're behind. The race is long, and in the end it's only with yourself - Phil, *The Big Kahuna*

I have a competition in me. I want no one else to succeed. I hate most people - Plainview, *There Will be Blood*

I admit I was jealous when I heard the tales they told me about him, not of the brilliant, little prodigy, but of his father who had taught him everything... my father did not care for music - Salieri, *Amadeus*

Ooooooh, I wish I was you! - C. D. Bales, *Roxanne*

In my experience those who do not like you fall into two categories: The stupid and the envious. The stupid will like you in five years, the envious, never - John Wilmot, *The Libertine*

Of course there's envy: why isn't my life like this? Sure I want their money and clothes and jobs and opinions - Rob, *High Fidelity*

We're lucky --Yeah --I mean, people should be envying us, you know. I envy us. Yeah. I do - David St. Hubbins, *This is Spinal Tap*

Envy

What we have looks pretty good until we see someone else with something better. Aristotle defined envy in *Rhetoric* "as the pain caused by the good fortune of others." Often envy involves more than just wanting to possess something; that really falls into the category of greed. Greedy people want stuff they don't have, while envious people resent the people who have the stuff they want.

Envy has been a theme in stories from ancient times. The Old Testament tells of Cain and Abel, Sarah and Hagar, Jacob and Esau, and Saul and David, among others. In Greek mythology Nemesis was the goddess of envy. She encourages retribution and indignation at undeserved good fortune. Envy can indeed be a nemesis for those of us who compare ourselves to others and have to compete. It can wreck those of us who seek status and validation at the expense of others. It can eat away at our integrity, and leave us feeling unsatisfied and incomplete. Envy can take the form of resentment, ambition, conformity, and competition.

Jealousy is about others, envy is about me

Envy and jealousy are not exactly the same thing. Envy is about possessing something someone else has. Jealousy is about protecting a relationship from someone or something that threatens it. In *Toy Story* Woody is both jealous and envious of Buzz Lightyear.

Woody is envious of Buzz because Buzz is "a cool toy." Buzz has features that make him the more exciting toy. Mr. Potato Head asks, "How come you don't come with a laser, Woody?" Woody feels his pull string is inadequate after looking at everything Buzz can do. Woody envies the status

Buzz has gained among the other toys and tries to belittle Buzz to his peers. For their part, perhaps the other toys envy Woody for being Andy's favorite, and somewhat enjoy his obvious insecurity at his loss of status.

Woody doesn't just resent losing the status of being Andy's favorite, he fears losing Andy's affection. Woody is afraid that Andy will forget about him and shift his affection to Buzz. Woody wants to be the toy that brings Andy the most pleasure, just as he has been in the past. Woody experiences a sense of loss and insecurity similar to a first child when a new baby is brought home.

In *Toy Story 2* we see this loss expressed again by Jessie, who is discarded when her owner Emily feels she has become too old for a doll. This is the greatest fear of any toy, that it will no longer serve the purpose for which it was created: to bring pleasure. But when it stops being about protecting relationships and becomes about protecting status, it becomes envy.

Resentment

Most of us also think life should be fair. We may develop a sense of entitlement in which we equate the opportunity to possess with the right to possess. Perhaps we compare ourselves with the people who have what we want and conclude that we've earned what they have. This sort of thinking leads to resentment and envy.

David Spade's character Richard, in *Tommy Boy*, is smart and hardworking. He resents the boss's son Tommy who has been given a job, an office, and, as Richard observes, "You have a window, and why shouldn't you, you have been here 10 minutes." It annoys Richard that someday Tommy will inherit the company, though he knows little and seems to care even less about the business. Even though Richard knows the business he lacks the people skills that are crucial to sales. Rather than trying to develop the interpersonal skills he lacks, Richard derides Tommy with comments like "Now I know you'd love to just sit there and keep being not slim, but we got to work a little today, OK?"

Richard's attitudes and reactions in *Tommy Boy* are similar to those of the Prodigal Son's brother in Jesus' parable. After squandering the inheritance his father advanced him the little brother comes home in disgrace, only to be welcomed with open arms by his father. The father throws a celebration like none given in that house before. Based on what the parable tells us the Prodigal's older brother is probably just as resentful when his loser brother shows up for work the next morning as Richard is of Tommy.

In *As Good as It Gets* Carol, Simon, and Melvin are on a road trip. All of them face issues that make their lives difficult. Carol, a waitress, is a single mother with a chronically ill child. Simon is a gay man who has been the victim of a beating and is traveling to see his parents who banished him from their home when he came out. Melvin is an obsessive-compulsive writer whose disorder makes it almost impossible to develop friendships.

As they discuss their problems Carol tries to put a positive spin on their situations saying, "OK, we all have these terrible stories to get over, and you…" Melvin interrupts, "It's not true. Some have great stories, pretty stories that take place at lakes with boats and friends and noodle salad. Just no one in this car. But, a lot of people, that's their story. Good times, noodle salad. What makes it so hard is not that you had it bad, but that you're pissed that so many others had it good." We ask "why me?" We see that life isn't fair. If we're one of the "haves" we may not notice, but if we are one of the "have nots" we definitely see the inequity and may resent the "haves."

Often envy arises from our sense of justice. If everyone is created equal then why do some people have more than others? Why are some people more talented, more financially blessed, more socially skilled? Why do some people seem to have greater opportunity? Why does society seem to assign some people more value than others? Why do some people seem to receive preferential treatment? Perhaps this inequality has led some of us to believe that blessing is some sort of limited commodity... and we don't feel like we're getting ours.

Maybe we think the universe is arbitrarily doling out good luck to some and bad luck to others. We may begin to judge others, trying to determine whether they deserve the good fortune that comes their way. Comparing ourselves to others is one way that bitterness can take root. We envy what we do not have and resent those who have it.

Ambition

Schadenfreude is a German word for the satisfaction we feel when another person suffers. This envious resentment probably explains the popularity of celebrity gossip shows. Many of us enjoy seeing famous people discredited. We perceive that these people are somehow our superiors and if we cannot be elevated to their level we want to see them come crashing down to ours.

In *The Lion King* Scar cannot see himself in second place. He plots to overthrow his brother's throne and takes delight in doing it. After proclaiming that he "just can't wait to be king" young Simba asks the innocent question, "Hey Uncle Scar, when I'm king, what will that make you?" For

Scar the answer is "not enough." The question nags at each, "who would I be without this status?"

If we believe that our status is what makes us valuable and important we are likely to become envious of anyone who diverts attention and glory away from us. Ambition makes us vulnerable to envy, pride, and fear.

In *Amadeus* composer Salieri is frustrated that he has to work so hard to write music that is, at best, average, while Mozart seems to write brilliant music effortlessly. He judges Mozart's lifestyle and feels Mozart doesn't deserve the talent he's been given. Before Mozart comes along Salieri appears humble and devoted to God, and probably feels very blessed that his career has led to his position at court. He also associates his religious devotion with his success, believing that God is rewarding him for being such a great Christian. Mozart's talent blows that theory out of the water. Mozart's self-absorbed, hedonistic lifestyle assaults Salieri's beliefs about how God works. He is shaken to his very core. Salieri is unwilling to accept God's wisdom in blessing Mozart with the greater talent.

In his bitterness Salieri tells God, "From now on we are enemies, You and I. Because You choose for Your instrument a boastful, lustful, smutty, infantile boy and give me for reward only the ability to recognize the incarnation. Because You are unjust, unfair, unkind, I will block You, I swear it. I will hinder and harm Your creature on earth as far as I am able." Ultimately Salieri's envy is fueled by both his ego and his sense of justice. He angrily tells a priest that he can "speak for all mediocrities in the world. I am their champion. I am their patron saint."

Envy is unavoidable when we expect rewards based on some imagined criteria of fairness. Salieri is under the impression that his piety should have earned him the talent and recognition Mozart receives. The writer of Ecclesiastes points out, "I have observed something else under the sun. The fastest runner doesn't always win the race, and the strongest warrior doesn't always win the battle. The wise sometimes go hungry, and the skillful are not necessarily wealthy. And those who are educated don't always lead successful lives. It is all decided by chance, by being in the right place at the right time" (Ecc. 9:11).

Conformity, competition, and validation

At the root of much envy is comparison and competition. We want to be the best and to have the best. If another person gains recognition for something we are also able to do we may tell ourselves, and maybe even others, that we could do a better job. We become resentful, believing that we are more deserving, or at least just as deserving of recognition and opportunity. This happens in families a lot. The Old Testament is full of examples of sibling rivalry: Cain and Abel, Jacob and Esau, Rachel and Leah, Joseph and his brothers.

In the movie *Little Giants* the O'Shea brothers coach opposing pee-wee football teams. The older brother Kevin is a Heisman trophy winner who is richer and more respected in the community than his brother Danny, who feels he's always lived in Kevin's shadow. In our culture athletic ability, especially among males, gains instant esteem for those who possess it. Among young boys, before money matters, before appearance matters, athletic talent can make a child king of the playground.

When teams are picked there are some kids who are always picked first and some kids who are always picked last. For some being picked last is not only a public acknowledgement that they are not talented in the area of sports, but an assignment of worth as a human being. In *Little Giants* a young Danny says, "Gee I must be pretty bad if my own brother won't pick me." He goes on to tell his older brother, "I stink. You're perfect and I stink. That's it. The End."

Danny carries this perception of himself into adulthood. The town has erected a gigantic billboard with Kevin's picture on it, touting him as a hometown hero. Danny has toiled away in obscurity in the same town, looking at that billboard and feeling inadequate. When Danny's daughter is cut from Kevin's team because she is a girl Danny identifies heavily with this rejection and forms a team of kids who do not have the physical attributes or resources usually associated with sports victors. After an ugly start Danny overcomes his own insecurity and finds ways to use whatever attributes or competencies each child possesses to better their chances of winning. Through this each member of the team comes to see his or her value as a contributor rather than feeling diminished because of lack of talent or ability.

Competition and conformity are so much a part of growing up. Boys who are athletic and girls who are beautiful receive an undue amount of esteem in early years. Children who do not fit into these categories may envy children who receive attention because of these attributes. This could be a reason that underdog team beats stereotypical alpha-male team is a popular formula for kids' sports movies. While the members of the underdog team are usually a representation of every type of child: the brain, the smart kid, the mouth, the insecure, the fat kid, minorities, and girls, the opposing team is usually made up of white males who are all athletic, fit, well-groomed, and good-looking. There is a vicarious satisfaction in seeing the sort of kids many of us envied as

Envy

children crushed by the rejects and disrespected.

We sometimes value people based on their ability to contribute to society. Various "end of the world" movies present a scenario in which only certain people are selected to survive. There is usually some sort of survival bunker, like the one in *Deep Impact*. A comet is hurtling toward earth, and when scientists and engineers fail to stop it a national lottery is employed to determine who gets to survive in the bunker. 800,000 will be picked at random, but 200,000 are "pre-selected" due to their value to society as doctors, artists, scientists, politicians, or for some other contribution. This idea of assigning worth is an intriguing aspect of *Deep Impact*. Many disaster films portray individuals choosing to sacrifice themselves for the good of many, but the idea that some are more worthy to live than others is not always so openly portrayed.

Leggo your Ego

Larry experiences frustration and envy toward Bob in *The Big Kahuna* when Bob blows an opportunity Larry is certain he would nail. Three salesmen are at a convention to sell lubricants. They prepare a party in their hospitality suite in hopes that Mr. Fuller, a big client, will come to their party. Larry and Phil are experienced salesmen who have been in the business for some time, while Bob is at his first convention. Making this contact is critical to their mission at the convention. As a sales representative, Larry's ambition is to land "The Big Kahuna" of clients, represented by Mr. Fuller.

In the course of the evening the new guy, Bob, unintentionally meets Mr. Fuller. He later explains to Larry and Phil that he talked to Fuller for some time but never mentioned their product or company. Instead they discussed God. This appalls Larry, who goes into a tirade about Bob's responsibility to the company. Larry is envious that Bob is in a position to make a sale he's spent his whole career chasing. He resents that Bob is the one with the contact, and is appalled that Bob has failed to represent the company that is financing his trip.

Bob feels that he would be insincere and manipulative to bring up business after the spiritual discussion he's had with Fuller. Bob, though he is a salesman sent to the convention to sell, places his idealism over obligations to his employer.

Larry has focused all his energy and compromised other areas of his life in order to rise in his career. Larry's entire sense of worth is tied up in the very thing that Bob so easily dismisses. For Larry, convincing someone to buy his product has nothing to do with the product. It is about his power to convince someone else to do something he wants them to do. Success in this area makes him feel important. It affirms his worth to himself.

Phil, the other salesman, feels used up. His marriage is in trouble; his enthusiasm for the job is waning. Phil is in a place where he is examining his life and thinking seriously about the person he wants to spend the rest of his life being. Phil knows there has to me more, and not only wants to find it for himself but wants Larry to find it as well. It is Phil who holds the wisdom that both Larry and Bob need to progress in their journeys. He has worked with Larry for years. He loves Larry and sees beneath his friend's jaded exterior.

It is interesting that Bob is the religious character in this movie but it is Phil who sees Larry as a person who needs redemption, while Bob merely condemns Larry for his vicious attitude. Phil sees past Larry's envy to the insecurity and lack of self-worth that drives it. Larry and Phil know that they are unsatisfied and are struggling to figure out where to go next. Bob sees his faith as moral superiority. He appears completely satisfied with his life, and states that he has nothing to regret.

Phil sees through Bob's seeming integrity to his point of need. "I'm saying you've already done plenty of things to regret, you just don't know what they are. It's when you discover them, when you see the folly in something you've done and you wish that you had it do over, but you know you can't, because it's too late. So you pick that thing up, and carry it with you to remind you that life goes on, the world will spin without you; you really don't matter in the end. Then you will gain character, because honesty will reach out from inside and tattoo itself across your face." Unfortunately Bob's lack of awareness and unexamined certainty presents a faith that, without the presence of regret, seems to lack compassion for Larry, and negates his own continuous need for redemption. Ultimately Bob's shallowness is revealed.

There is no villain in this movie, only three fallen men who need redemption. Phil's ability to help the other two see one another is the beginning of addressing both Larry's envy and Bob's shallowness. At the heart of this movie is the truth that none of us is good enough, so there is no reason to envy anyone. All of us are hurting and fallen. It is easier to judge people we think of as rivals.

Envy separates us from others. Instead of recognizing that we all experience need as part of the human condition, envy convinces us that others have attained what we have not. It directs our attention and focus toward other people, their status, or their stuff. Envy leads to a lack of contentment. This lack of contentment causes us to turn inward. We lose interest in our neighbor's welfare and become competitive instead.

In 1 Corinthians 13 Paul says that love "does not seek its own and is not envious." If we express thanks it is usually for what we have, but seldom do we offer thanks for other's blessings. We may wish them well and pray for them when something goes wrong, but generally, when it comes to provision, our thankfulness is about what we have and our petitions are about what we think we still need.

Others-centeredness

In *Elizabethtown* Drew Baylor has experienced a "fiasco" in his professional life and concludes that "Success, not greatness, was the only god the whole world served." When his failure comes crashing down, the friends, the girl, the props and perks of success are gone. Somewhere in his "pursuit of greatness" he has disengaged himself from his family, and now it's too late to recover the time he lost with his dad. He feels lost and embarrassed as he flies to Kentucky to retrieve his father's body and meet his Baylor relatives.

Flight attendant Claire Colburn intervenes in the life of Drew Baylor. Unsolicited, she strikes up conversation with him and, from the moment they meet, Claire senses Drew's need and his grief. Even though he does not initially tell her that his father has died, she picks up on it because she is paying attention to Drew rather than to herself. She senses his loss, and responds with warmth and friendship. As their relationship progresses she offers her love and support, not only as he deals with the death of his father, but with his other issues as well.

At one point Claire confesses to Drew that she is "a substitute person." She is available even though she knows that ultimately she is not first choice. Although she says being a substitute person is less pressure, like all of us, she really does want to be special. Drew tells her that she deserves better. What is remarkable about her attitude is her motive. It doesn't seem to come from insecurity so much as from another revelation she makes about herself. "I can't help helping." She is willing to allow herself to be there, to be transparent, demanding nothing in return, because someone needs her. Claire has a servant's heart.

Claire's response to Drew's explanation of his monumental business failure is, "so what?" She separates his value as a person from money or success. Because she does not envy, Claire has a hard time understanding Drew's extreme reaction to losing his company a billion dollars. She has a hard time understanding why this would be a reason for others to reject him. Sensing that Drew needs to deal with his issues, Claire pours herself into creating a road trip for Drew in order to bring healing. "I want you to get into the deep, beautiful, melancholy of everything that's happened." She lets him go because he needs to go. She puts herself in the position to be rejected. She is more interested in his healing than in her own desires.

Selfishness and ego are wrapped up in envy. If we weren't so self-involved we wouldn't be so aware of everything we think we're lacking. It is ego and envy that leads us to compare ourselves with other people. Others-centered people look at others and rejoice when they are blessed.

Supportive relationships

In the *Lord of the Rings* Sam and Frodo seek the best for one another. Sam joins Frodo on his journey to destroy the ring of power. Because he is Frodo's friend he faces down the powerful elf Elrond saying, "Frodo's not going anywhere without me." He isn't ashamed to identify himself as Frodo's gardener when Faramir asks if he's the bodyguard. Sam never wants to be a hero, in fact he wonders at finding himself a player in a heroic tale. He accepts his role for the sake of his friend and his ideals. Sam believes "Folk in those stories had lots of chances of turning back, only they didn't. They kept going. Because they were holding on to something.... That there's some good in this world, Mr. Frodo... and it's worth fighting for."

He could have resented playing sidekick to Frodo, but Sam's unwavering goal is to support Frodo. At one point in the last movie Frodo tells Sam, "I need you on my side," to which Sam responds, "I'm on your side, Mr. Frodo." In one of the final scenes Sam carries Frodo up Mount Doom because Frodo can't go on, but won't let Sam carry the ring. Though he recognizes the importance of their mission to defeat evil and destroy the ring, Sam is primarily motivated by love and loyalty. This sort of love between friends is selfless. Each only desires good for the other.

What love is

Forrest Gump lacks the egotism that is necessary for self-seeking or envy. He accepts each person, and delights in that person's success and happiness. Forrest looks outside himself. Forrest is constantly concerned about the happiness and well-being of others. Those surrounding him are dissatisfied. Lieutenant Dan wanted to die heroically in combat, not end up in a wheelchair. Jenny wanted to be famous and make a difference, but ends up a stripper. Forrest becomes famous and successful at everything he does. He accidentally ends up participating in many historic events, but it is the people in his life who matter to him rather than his success or influence on history.

Envy

He loves Jenny sacrificially, willing to forgo being with her if she is happier being somewhere else or happier being with someone else. He never judges her. He just loves her. He loves his friends. He honors his fallen friend Bubba by following through with the shrimp business they planned together. He reaches out to the wounded Lieutenant Dan even though Dan insults and rejects him. He continues to encourage Dan and expects him to eventually find his way. Forrest Gump may have been mentally retarded but his heart is remarkably mature and his priorities more in order than most of the characters in the movie.

Jenny does not understand this when she tells Forrest, "You don't know what love is." She is looking at love as a way to satisfy passion or find fulfillment. Forrest knows exactly what love is; it's not about himself. "Love is patient and kind. Love is not jealous or boastful or proud or rude. It does not demand its own way. It is not irritable, and it keeps no record of being wronged. It does not rejoice about injustice but rejoices whenever the truth wins out. Love never gives up, never loses faith, is always hopeful, and endures through every circumstance" (I Cor. 13:4-6).

We need to feel that we are adequate, that what we have and what we do is adequate. God makes us enough. We will never be enough without him, and are always enough with him. It is in him that we "live and move and exist" (Acts 17:28a), and this existence in him is the validation for our lives.

7 PRIDE

Vanity is definitely my favorite sin. So basic. Self-love, the all-natural opiate - John Milton, *The Devil's Advocate*

What is it with men and asking for directions? - Dory, *Finding Nemo*

Remember boys, there's no points for second place - Slider, *Top Gun*

The power, feels good... But you lose yourself to it... - Peter Parker, *Spiderman*

Mr. Corleone never asks a second favor once he's refused the first, understood? - Tom Hayden, *The Godfather*

You know, you should play with Dr. Beeper and myself. I mean, he's been club champion for three years running and I'm no slouch myself - Judge Smails, *Caddyshack*

What do all men with power want? More power - The Oracle, *The Matrix*

Pride

Some are more beautiful. Some have better stuff. Some are naturally gifted in particular areas. Knowing this is not pride. It would be a pretentious humility to deny our unique set of gifts and talents. Everyone likes having accomplishments and talents noticed. There is a positive side to pride that drives us to seek perfection, care about quality, and inspire others to greatness as well.

When we begin to believe our own hype, self-respect can lapse into self-importance and pride. Our pride might be evident to others as egotism, pretentiousness, arrogance, and hubris, but we are unlikely to recognize it as a flaw.

Egotism

The obnoxious Gaston in *Beauty and the Beast* is both vain and offensive. Gaston believes he is the epitome of perfect manhood. He sees Belle as an appropriate appendage rather than a real person. He wants a trophy wife and has no doubt that Belle will consider it an honor to marry him. He and his friends are totally shocked when she turns him down. "No one says 'no' to Gaston!" sing Gaston and his shocked friends.

His friends admire him and have built him up so much that none of them can see his faults. His friends sing, "There's no man in town as admired as you. You're ev'ryone's favorite guy… No one's slick as Gaston. No one's quick as Gaston… Perfect, a pure paragon!"

Sometimes we can contribute to the development of a vain disposition by heaping too much praise, admiration, or status on someone, especially if it is unearned. Once we gain status we may be tempted to pretend we are more capable or influential than we actually are in order to maintain the position. This can lead to awkward social situations, such as Gaston's constant proposals to Belle.

In *My Cousin Vinny* inexperienced lawyer Vincent Gambini comes to the rescue when his cousin and a friend are wrongfully accused of a murder in Alabama. He gives phony credentials to the judge and tries to finesse his way through the case. Vinny soon realizes he is totally unprepared for courtroom procedures. When his fiancée Lisa tries to help him by reading the law books that he should have already researched, Vinny gets defensive and won't listen to her.

Later Lisa takes some pictures of the crime scene which he dismisses as useless. This injures her pride. When those pictures and Lisa's expertise become critical to his case Vinny must swallow his pride in a hilarious scene in which he puts the still-angry Lisa on the witness stand as a hostile witness.

After the trial Vinny is quiet and not as happy as he should be about the victory, so Lisa asks, "So what's your problem?" He tells her "My problem is, I wanted to win my first case without any help from anybody." She responds, "You know, this could be a sign of things to come. You win all your cases, but with somebody else's help, right? You win case after case, and then afterwards you have to go up to somebody and you have to say 'thank you'."

We can become more concerned with the roles we play in a project than in the success of the project itself. Like Lisa we may want to make sure our contributions are recognized, or like Vinny we may not want to share glory. Either way, becoming egotistical can derail a project. "This is not about me" may be the most important starting point for accomplishing a task or contributing to a project.

Pretension

Pride prevents us from being authentic. We might feel the need to conform to some sort of ideal, real or imagined. Perhaps we gain confidence and self-satisfaction when we feel that we are doing the "right things" correctly. When others notice our efforts we feel even better. Eventually how we look doing life becomes more important than life itself.

The relationship between Elizabeth Bennett and Mr. Darcy in *Pride and Prejudice* has a bumpy start when each forms a negative first impression. Both are prideful about their personal integrity and their abilities to read other people, so neither wants to admit misjudging the other. And, nobody likes to be misjudged, so both have difficulty in forgiving the other… especially since no one apologizes.

Social events throw them together and they eventually see one another's best qualities, but there is always tension between them. Elizabeth struggles with embarrassment because of her family's poverty and because her mother and two of her sisters are openly concerned with social climbing and making "good" marriages. While Mr. Darcy has valid concerns about protecting his family from gold diggers his assumption that Elizabeth falls into this category wounds her pride. Although she always tries to behave with integrity she cannot help feeling that her family is a reflection on her character.

Although Mr. Darcy sees Elizabeth's great qualities, he cannot let go of his pretension. In his class-conscious proposal he says, "I have fought against my better judgment, my family's expectations, the inferiority of your birth by rank and circumstance. All these things I am willing to put aside and ask you to end my agony." Naturally this snobbery does not sit well with Elizabeth. Although *Pride and*

Prejudice is considered a period piece, the idea that power or wealth somehow makes us superior is as relevant today as it was in the nineteenth century. There is still plenty of pretension and exclusivity in the social arenas of the 21st century. People who receive lots of admiration or hold lots of power can develop an inflated sense of their own importance.

In *The Devil Wears Prada* Miranda Priestly sweeps into the office and dumps her coat and purse on the desk of one of her assistants, both of whom she calls Emily. She makes demands like, "Find me that piece of paper I had in my hand yesterday morning." To her credit, Miranda is fixated on putting out a great magazine. In her pride she considers herself irreplaceable. Her distrust of everyone else's judgment but her own and her overbearing attitude alienate her from her colleagues and employees.

Fear is Miranda's primary management method. She manipulates her employees by giving and withdrawing trust and approval in order to get them to do whatever she requires. Miranda speaks in an affected near-whisper, expressing her deep disappointment and questioning the worth of those who fail her.

Her behavior is a reflection of her belief that maintaining distance retains power. She is feared, somewhat admired, but not loved. Miranda's pride causes her to insulate herself from the people around her. Ultimately she experiences professional success at the expense of her marriage and friendships.

Eventually her protégé Andrea realizes how alone Miranda really is. At about the same time it dawns upon Andrea that, while she is not as mean-spirited as Miranda, she is making the same relationship sacrifices. Andrea is willing to admit her mistake and make the necessary changes to get back on course. Miranda seems to recognize Andrea's escape, but her pride will not allow her to let go of the life that is making her miserable, because it makes her feel so important.

Pride makes "I'm sorry" stick to the roof of our mouths. It creates a sense of entitlement in which "thank you" doesn't come naturally. We don't think to apologize because we're pretty sure we're in the right, and that the other party in some way caused the problem. We don't think to be grateful because we're pretty sure we're responsible for the blessing, or if we didn't actually earn it we're entirely deserving of it.

Arrogance

Pride also manifests itself as arrogance. *Die Hard* gives us three characters who believe they are smarter than the average bear: the mastermind Hans Gruber, the independent New York cop John McClane, and the 80's corporate stereotype Harry Ellis. When uber villain Hans Gruber and his accomplices take a group of co-workers hostage in an office tower on Christmas Eve, Hans' well laid plans are thwarted by New York cop John McClane.

Hans becomes even more frustrated when his fellow criminals are less competent than he expected. He prides himself in developing a creative and effective plan. He enjoys the power he yields over his hostages, the authorities, and his accomplices. Hans describes his expectations, "I wanted this to be professional. Efficient, adroit, cooperative, not a lot to ask." Hans always believes he is the smartest person in the room, and has a sarcastic put down for everyone. He underestimates John McClane. The result of his arrogance is a great illustration of the proverb, "Pride goes before destruction, and haughtiness before a fall" (Prov. 16:18). And

Pride

if you've seen the movie, this verse is doubly appropriate.

John McClane sees himself as a pretty basic guy. He's persistent and possesses great problem-solving skills. He's a cop. He is almost arrogantly certain that his read on the situation is correct. He's so certain he's right that he is willing to challenge local and federal law enforcement authorities.

John struggles with pride in his relationship with his wife, who has chosen her career over their marriage. But the biggest indication that pride is an issue for John is his delicious sarcasm. Like Hans, John's sarcastic one-liners indicate his lack of respect for the intelligence of those he has to deal with.

Hans and John seem to be the most capable and knowledgeable characters in the movie. They find it difficult to accomplish their respective tasks, crime and crime-fighting, because they feel they are surrounded by idiots. Hans does not consider John enough of a threat because Hans is convinced he is too smart to fail. John does not underestimate Hans. He knows he might fail, and this bit of humility gives him the edge he needs.

Ellis, on the other hand, overestimates his own intelligence and underestimates his captors'. Ellis is so intent on proving his own ability to play with the big boys that he fails to recognize that Hans' own pride should not be challenged. It quickly becomes apparent that Ellis is in over his head, but he refuses to accept that assessment from John.

Ellis seriously miscalculates Hans, saying, "Business is business. You use a gun, I use a fountain pen. What's the difference?" Unfortunately for Ellis fountain pens aren't nearly as lethal as guns, and his arrogance escalates the situation and puts more people in danger. It is arrogant to think that any of us can fully control a situation in which people are making choices that counter one another's purposes. In some situations it is prudent to be "wise as serpents and gentle as doves" (Matt. 10:16b). Arrogance can keep us from exercising wisdom and restraint.

Disaster movies also serve as reminders that we cannot control everything. Movies like *Twister, Deep Impact, Armageddon, Dante's Peak,* and *Volcano* serve as reminders that we may be able to use what we know to deal with forces of nature, but we cannot prevent them. *The Happening* and *Day After Tomorrow* address the attitude that we are immune from possible consequences of our choices as a society, while *Deep Blue Sea* and *I Am Legend* speak to the arrogance that can accompany science. It is prideful to become overly certain of our own ability to manipulate creation.

In *I Am Legend* doctors find a cure for cancer through genetic engineering. The doctors use a virus known for being unpredictable and prone to mutation, and make premature decisions about distributing the vaccine they develop. A majority of the people whom they immunize react negatively to the vaccine. They lose their minds, wandering the streets at night, killing and devouring any life they find. Those not affected flee the cities, living in small, heavily guarded communities.

Robert Neville, one of the doctors responsible for the vaccine, is intent on finding a way to reverse the effects. Throughout the movie Neville is confronted with messages like "God still loves us" in shop windows and on walls. A woman and her son appear and save Neville's life. She insists that God has sent her and that Neville is going to save the world, but Neville, disillusioned by the failure of his cancer cure and the horrors it causes, proclaims "There is no God!"

Pride

He is certain that if this nightmare is to end it will be because he as a scientist can fix the problem he helped create. Neville eventually accepts that he may not be able to overcome this enormous problem alone.

I am Legend struggles with the question of who is responsible for the consequences of mankind's conceit and who is responsible for fixing those consequences. It explores God's role when tragedies occur. The more knowledge and power we have the more we may believe that we can manipulate the world around us to our own purposes.

Hubris

Even with the best of intentions we sometimes overstep our positions as politicians, medical professional, teachers, or any other field that affords authority. Pride can convince us that a position of leadership or power gives us the right, maybe even the obligation, to play God. This sort of excessive arrogance is called hubris.

In *The Mission* conflict arises when a group of missionaries challenge the hubris of politicians and church authorities over the well-being of the Guanari tribe. As missionaries work to teach the Guanari about Christ's love, their missions are pawns in a negotiation between the church and Portugal. Cardinal Altamirano is sent by the church to determine which seven missions to close.

Nowhere in Altamirano's purposes is the conversion of the Guanari. Altamirano's attitude reflects a belief that the church itself is more important than its primary purpose. It also reflects the general conceit of 17th century European settlers that all land inhabited by non-Europeans is basically uninhabited, regardless of native societies which may live there.

Roman Catholics believe that the hierarchy of the church holds the authority of Christ, so rejecting this authority is a much bigger deal for Gabriel and the priests at the mission than it might seem. All of them understand that the Church as an institution is at odds with what they understand the Church as Christ's body to be. When it becomes clear that the missions are going to be closed, by force if necessary, and that the Guanari will be taken as slaves, they choose to challenge the church.

Rodrigo, a former slave trader turned priest, and some of the other priests prepare to defend the mission by force. When urged to fight Gabriel refuses, "If might is right, then love has no place in the world. It may be so, it may be so. But I don't have the strength to live in a world like that, Rodrigo." Instead, he gathers like-minded Guanari for a final mass. All of them recognize that their efforts will most likely fail.

On learning their fate the conflicted Cardinal sits down to write a letter to the Pope. One of his aides says, "You had no alternative. We must work in the world and the world is thus," to which he replies, "No... Thus have we made the world... Thus have I made it." He realizes that atrocities in the name of "authority" are not inevitable, yet he concludes, "I did what I had to do given a legitimate purpose." Hubris sometimes causes leadership to lose compassion and to legitimize their actions in the name of "necessity."

Most of us want to think of ourselves as honorable and want to believe that when we assert our authority it is for noble purpose. Most of us want to believe in our own integrity and may lie to ourselves and others in order to keep up that pretense.

In *Batman: The Dark Knight* the Joker takes aim at this attitude with a pride that is stripped of pretension. Alfred tries to explain the Joker to Batman, saying "Some men

Pride

aren't looking for anything logical, like money. They can't be bought, bullied, reasoned, or negotiated with. Some men just want to watch the world burn."

The Joker is entertained by others' fear, and is energized by the power he experiences through attacking another's self-image. Even the crooks in Batman can't understand the Joker. They commit crimes for gain but the Joker does it to "introduce a little anarchy, upset the established order." The Joker not only enjoys hurting others, he enjoys manipulating them so that they abandon their moral compasses.

He believes "in their last moments, people show you who they really are." In a moment of fear, many of us lose our vanity, or our integrity, or both. The joker revels in the power he has to bring people to this moment. He cynically insists that no one will uphold values, and claims that society proves his philosophy, "See, I'm not a monster... I'm just ahead of the curve." He believes those who act on their selfish desires are simply being authentic.

Batman sees that his own crime-fighting, while it accomplishes good, is full of secrecy and compromise. He questions his own motives and struggles with Joker's challenge that his "good" is really "evil." That Harvey Dent turns and becomes Two-Face seems to prove the Joker right. Batman is left wondering if his role as "silent guardian and watchful protector" is really the solution to Gotham's decline.

While on the surface Batman's choices seem noble, the Joker forces him to question his motives and his methods. When Batman takes the fall for Two-Face, those who know the truth allow the people of Gotham to believe he is guilty. Believing that their positions as leaders give them the responsibility and the right to filter the truth raises several questions: Is it appropriate for leaders to withhold information from the public? Does this indicate a lack of trust in the judgment and intelligence of the public? Is it hubris when leadership lies to those we lead?

Humility

Humility does not rob us of self-respect but confers value in relation to God and others. It relieves us of the need to prove our superiority or worth. It implies respect for God, for others, and for self.

A prideful person asks questions like "How does this affect me?" while the humble person asks "How can I help?" Pride is always looking for the personal advantage while humility understands priorities. Humility involves a willingness to put purpose before personality and others before self.

Purpose before personality

The Lord of the Rings movies chronicle the pursuit of power. Boromir, Saruman, and Gollum all fall for the lure of power and personal importance that the ring offers. Pride makes all these characters vulnerable to evil.

In contrast, Frodo and Sam exhibit humility in their quest to destroy the ring. In Middle Earth one would expect elves, wizards, or men to be the ones to defeat Sauron. It is their strengths that make them vulnerable to the ring of power. Instead, the powers at work in that world choose a lowly Hobbit. Paul suggests to the Corinthians that "God chose things the world considers foolish in order to shame those who think they are wise. And he chose things that are powerless to shame those who are powerful" (I Cor. 1:27).

Pride

Accomplishment through our own wisdom and power often leads to egotism and self-promotion. For the Hobbits the important thing is the task that needs to be accomplished rather than who gets it done and what glory, power, or riches might result.

In many stories it is in the companion, the side-kick, that we find what C. S. Lewis called "the load, or weight, or burden of my neighbor's glory." He called this "a load so heavy that only humility can carry it." The idea is that "the dullest and most uninteresting person you talk to may one day be a creature which, if you saw it now, you would be strongly tempted to worship, or else a horror and a corruption such as you now meet, if at all, only in a nightmare."

Members of the *Lord of the Rings* bear the weight of glory. Sam carries Frodo when Frodo can no longer go on. Aragorn puts aside his claim as king in an attempt to restore the citizens of Gondor. Frodo reaches out to Gollum with compassion, hoping to rescue him from his obsession with the ring. Bilbo is spared Gollum's fate because Gandalf intervenes, and the elves at Rivendell bring healing to his mind. Support has a profound effect on success.

In order to be humble we have to stop wanting to be the starring attraction. Humble people choose principles above self-promotion. Humility is about seeing ourselves in perspective, and being honest about our abilities, our contributions, and, most of all, our power.

Others-centered humility

"Did you really come here with Lloyd Dobler? How did that happen?" asks a fellow senior in *Say Anything* when beautiful, brainy, successful Diane shows up to their graduation party with an unlikely date. Everyone likes Lloyd but nobody expects much from him. It is doubtful that Lloyd and Diane match up on eHarmony's 27 levels of compatibility.

He is willing to serve as the "keymaster" at parties in order to keep people from driving drunk. He is protective of his friends when they are hurt. Lloyd says he's looking for "a dare to be great situation" that has little to do with wealth, power, or success as the world defines it. People think he's headed for mediocrity and Lloyd is okay with that. Paul told the Philippians: "Don't be selfish; don't try to impress others. Be humble, thinking of others as better than yourselves. Don't look out only for your own interests, but take an interest in others, too" (Phil 2:3-4).

When Diane's dad Jim asks about his future Lloyd says, "I don't want to sell anything, buy anything, or process anything as a career. I don't want to sell anything bought or processed, or buy anything sold or processed, or repair anything sold, bought, or processed. You know, as a career, I don't want to do that." This may sound like adolescent conceit to the millions of us who do whatever it is we do in order to pay the bills, but Lloyd seems to be driven more by idealism than by pride. He is unwilling to be someone he is not, even to impress a girl's father.

Later Lloyd finishes answering the question, "What I really want to do with my life - what I want to do for a living - is I want to be with your daughter. I'm good at it." He is content to provide encouragement and support in order to help Diane reach her potential. Depending upon one's social philosophy many women experience either admiration or disrespect for making this same sort of choice. Lloyd's supporting role is not viewed as a valuable contribution, and the fact that he is a man makes it an even harder choice for others to accept.

Self-respect

Not all pride is sin. Many languages have two words to describe pride. One is for self-respect while an entirely different word is used for vanity. We practice self-respect when we contribute our best efforts, behave ethically, and recognize that we are part of something larger than ourselves.

Remember the Titans deals with three aspects of pride which can be positive: racial pride, team membership, and personal honor. Coach Yost's pride is hurt when he is passed over to become head coach of a high school team in the 1970's. Herman Boone, who is black, has been given the position for political reasons. Coach Yost discovers that his personal honor is more important than prejudice, accolades, or being in charge.

Coach Boone knows he is up for the job and understands that his performance will provide opportunities for other black coaches in the future. At first he is prideful and unwilling to seek advice from the other coaches. He sometimes displays stubbornness when his methods or ideas are challenged. Eventually Coach Boone sees that his personal pride is getting in the way of winning, so he redirects his pride away from himself and begins to build pride in the team.

Coach Boone inspires the players to take pride in themselves as a team. Their unity becomes as much a source of pride as their individual athletic abilities or the final score of the game. As team members they learn to display dignity and self-respect rather than arrogance or conceit. Producing good work is positive pride. Doing our best displays respect for the God who gives us our talents, the mentors who help us develop them, our loved ones who support our efforts, and the people who benefit from what we do.

Many people spend entirely too much time and money on appearances, but there is nothing wrong with taking pride in appearance out of self-respect, respect for those around us, and respect for the events we attend. There has to be a healthy balance in which we make fashion choices that express our personal style in an approachable way. Makeover shows like *What Not to Wear* and *How Do I Look?* follow real people on a journey toward self-confidence. Jesus said, "Consider the lilies of the field. Solomon in all his glory was not clothed like one of these." Seeing ourselves as God's lilies gives us the freedom to express individual beauty in a way that will not distract those around us as we turn our attention to more important issues than how we look.

We all like to feel important because we all actually *are* important. Equally important. The message of Christ is that each of us matter to him, and that he wants to have a relationship with each of us. We should feel important, just not *more* important. Each of us is special and unique, just like everybody else.

Some of the skills and knowledge that we hold up as critical to success fail to address the eternal questions of life. Humility is realizing that we might not even know what we think we know. We need to keep asking who God is, because He gets bigger every time we ask. We need to keep wondering how "love your neighbor" looks in each circumstance we face because love stretches us each time we exhibit it. In every challenge we face, for every person we meet, we need to keep asking how grace is manifested by God and what we are supposed to bring to the table. In interacting with others, humble people seek to do justly, love mercy, and walk humbly with our God (Micah 6:8).

We're all heroes if you catch us at the right moment - Andy Garcia, *Hero*

The further you run from your sins, the more exhausted you are when they catch up to you - Dalton Russell, *Inside Man*

You wear a mask for so long, you forget who you were beneath it - Dietrich, *V for Vendetta*

We must remember that all these things, the nuances, the anomalies, the subtleties, which we assume only accessorize our days, are in fact here for a much larger and nobler cause. They are here to save our lives - Karen Eiffel, *Stranger than Fiction*

What I want to do and what I do are two separate things. If we went around always doing what we want, there'd be chaos - *Simon Birch*

We have all got both light and dark inside us. What matters is the power we choose to act on. That's who we really are - Sirius Black, *Harry Potter and the Order of the Phoenix*

I'd like to quit thinking of the present as some minor insignificant preamble to something else - Cynthia Dunn, *Dazed and Confused*

CONCLUSION

In *Spaceballs* Darth Helmet says, "Evil will always triumph because good is dumb." Selfless choices go unappreciated, and most of the time cause us inconvenience and pain. Looking out for ourselves often seems like the smartest choice we can make. Sometimes all of us are villains.

In movies we see the good little angel and the evil little devil appear on a character's shoulder, to try to convince him or her to choose right or wrong. We relate to this tension between sin and virtue because all of us struggle with conflicting interests and conflicted spirits. Oddly, feeding either the villain or the hero can create feelings of empowerment and satisfaction.

Our inner villain might say that acting on selfish impulse is only natural. We're only being true to ourselves. Often we consider whether our actions or attitudes really hurt anyone but ourselves, and factor that in as well.

We may hear our inner hero saying, "Control yourself," or "Do the right thing," or "Think about who this might hurt," while our desires scream "Do it!" If we're honest, we probably think about the advantages and rewards we are likely to enjoy as well. That is the conflict that the seven deadly sins impose on our lives.

We've all been on the receiving end of one of the seven deadly sins. Perhaps we've been objectified by lust, ignored by sloth, or robbed by greed. We know how it feels to be hurt by anger. We see and feel the damage envy, gluttony, or pride can cause. We may understand and regret the hurt we cause, yet find it difficult to choose others' needs over satisfying our selfish tendencies.

Regret

In *Atonement* Briony Tallis tells a lie about her sister Cecelia and Cecelia's boyfriend Robbie. Briony's envy is the motivation that sets events in motion, yet *Atonement* is not really about envy, but about regret. The immediate results of Briony's lie are that she receives attention and sympathy, while Cecelia and Robbie are parted. She regrets her lie when she sees how much she's hurt two people she loves. She can't bring herself to confess her lie to her parents so she sticks with her story, unable to foresee the enormous consequences of this decision.

Events unfold in such a way that Briony is never able to apologize and receive forgiveness from those she wronged. Unable to make it right with them, she spends the rest of her life trying to pay for the pain she caused. Ultimately, as she grows old and guilt weighs heavier on her, Briony tells still more lies to relieve her guilt. She also denies herself the life she had hoped for, to atone for ruining Cecelia and Robbie's lives.

Atonement raises the question of whether we can really "make up" for our sins. Are acts of contrition, those things we do to relieve our consciences, not also selfish acts as well if we are doing them to make ourselves feel better? Briony seeks resolution by trying to create a happy ending for

Conclusion

Cecelia and Robbie. She tells others her fabrication as if it were the truth. She tries to make that their story, rather than the tragic reality that her lie set into motion.

Justice and Mercy

When we realize we've caused hurt most of us feel regret and experience guilt. Usually there is only so much we can do to fix the damage. As much as we may wish we could change history, the consequences of our actions tend to stick with us. Often the fallout extends to those we love as well.

If we are among those in the fallout of someone else's destructive choices we tend to hope that "what goes around comes around." Most of us enjoy seeing the "bad guys" pay for the misery they create for others. But when we are the villain in a situation we prefer the adage "forgive and forget." Grace becomes much more attractive than judgment when we are the ones repenting!

Of course, we should seek forgiveness from those we hurt. We also need to forgive ourselves and ask God to help us move on. Whether we're on the giving or receiving end of sin and forgiveness, we all tend to carry some baggage. This is the destructive nature of sin.

As human beings we try to make sense of the good and evil in ourselves and in each other. In spite of grumblings that our culture has no moral compass, in most stories we tend to root for the good guy, unless there is no good guy, or unless the good guy is irritatingly "holier than thou." We will also root for a character that arouses our sense of justice, even if he's an antagonist rather than a hero.

In a movie like *Se7en* we may be horrified by the crimes, but feel little compassion for the victims. After all, they each are guilty of one of the sins. We may be repelled by John

Doe, yet his twisted, ironic justice can feel strangely satisfying. We experience this detached sense of justice until Detective Mills, a character we know and care about, is affected. Only then are we willing to discard justice for mercy. The ending of *Se7en* makes the audience complicit with John Doe, if we, like Mills, judge his victims' sins without recognizing our own.

Villains and Heroes

Our own villainous tendencies sometimes overwhelm our heroic intentions. We all want to feel confident and secure, to believe our needs are met, that we are competent to meet those needs, and that we are "good" people. We spend much of our lives trying to insure that we keep feeling this way about ourselves.

Call him Satan, the devil, Lucifer, or any of his many names, this malevolent presence is no fiction, and evil originates with him. He is in the business of diverting us from God, and getting us to focus on ourselves is the most effective tactic in his arsenal. There is no need for overt evil if people simply self-destruct.

In the presence of evil we experience fear. If we're on the receiving end of some act of selfish aggression we rush to shield our emotions, our assets, or our lives. If we are the aggressors we are usually motivated by some overwhelming sense of need. Either way, we fear pain and loss. Our fear for ourselves leads us into temptation.

We may be afraid that we won't be happy if we're good. We fear that our dreams will be compromised by self-sacrifice. The desire to experience pleasure and avoid pain drives us to accept the seven deadly sins as viable methods for seeking satisfaction.

Conclusion

The difference between a hero and a villain is motivation. Fears, insecurities, and self-absorption lead to sin. Each of us finds consolation and satisfaction differently, so different sins will motivate us. We become used to feeding our needs by acting on these motivations. Sin tricks us into feeling safer when we're selfish.

We may long for the opportunity to be heroes, yet we cling to safety that never allows for heroics. Jesus said that "if you give up your life for me, you will find it" (Matt. 10:39b). We settle for trying to fix behavior, rather than seeking to become differently motivated. Author Antoine de Saint-Exupery said, "If you want to build a ship, don't drum up people to collect wood and don't assign them tasks and work, but rather teach them to long for the endless immensity of the sea."

God reveals his nature in our heroic longings, and makes his nature available to us through his Son. Too often our religious experiences assign us tasks to atone for our failures or urge us to follow and enforce rules out of fear rather than teaching us to long for the nature of Christ. He calls us to embrace aspects of his nature that oppose sin, and to be transformed.

Telling stories

"He has planted eternity in the human heart" (Ecc. 3:10), which causes us to desire love, kindness, and mercy, not only for ourselves but also for the society in which we live. His image in us compels us to admire the virtues and be repelled by the sins in the lives of others, even though our own lives sometimes tell a different story. God gives us sense enough to recognize the sins are destructive, so we learn how to rationalize, ignore, or normalize them.

God actually is everywhere, including in our creative moments. Movies, songs, art, mythologies, religions, psychological theories, and social conventions are all ways we as human beings try to investigate our nature. We examine good and evil in ourselves and in each other. Often elements of truth are contained in these creations because they are born of this common "eternal heart." God is always trying to show us his nature and invite us into his story.

C. S. Lewis wrote that "Miracles are a retelling in small letters of the very same story which is written across the whole world in letters too large for some of us to see." In God's hands each of our stories become less predictable and more real. The story he invites us into is not always safe or sanitary. It is full of loose ends and unresolved questions and deliberate belief. He invites us to see everything deeply, and experience everything intensely. He invites us to be forgiven when we fail. He invites us to replace the fears and sins that divert us with his transforming love. We begin to develop the vision to filter life experiences through his light, to gasp in wonder and to dance with abandon. Personal transformation is a miracle that reflects the large-lettered miracle of redemption.

Redemption and transformation

In *Gran Torino* Walt Kowalski is both a hero and a villain. He does not set out to be either. He simply responds to situations without filtering his basic nature. He sees the materialistic selfishness in his family but fails to recognize that the pride and anger in his own approach is self-centered as well.

Forming relationships with Sue, Thai, and Father Janovich causes Walt to become more aware of other

Conclusion

people. He begins using his talent for fixing things for the good of others. His involvement leads him to face his own crisis differently because he allows himself into relationships in which he is affected by the needs of others.

He needs and experiences forgiveness and redemption, yet remains somewhat graceless, even in his newfound state of grace. His behavior and his heart are in the process of change, but this change is not presented as a moment of absolute clarity. Walt continues to be a gruff and somewhat spiteful man whose speech is peppered with racist slurs. The difference is that Walt is learning to love his neighbors, and to be motivated by that love.

Eventually Walt is challenged to affirm his intellectual morality with his hands and heart. Love motivates Walt to defeat the evil that threatens those he loves in such a way that he is not complicit with that evil. Rather than fixing the problem with vengeance, Walt is inspired to *become* the solution. Walt is something of a Christ figure in this movie. He changes the lives of his neighbors, and sacrifices himself in the process.

The process of transformation in Walt's story is cut short by his selfless decision to step into Thai and Sue's stories. John tells us that the greatest love is demonstrated by someone who "lays down his life for his friends" (John 15:13 NIV). Walt is still the same imperfect guy, but his acceptance of this unexpected relationship and his willingness to accept the risks and sacrifices that love sometimes requires results in profound change.

Even sad or dark endings can be satisfying if they make some sort of moral sense. Just as most of us want a satisfying resolution at the end of a story, we want our own internal conflicts resolved. In a movie it is comforting to see problems solved and relationships restored in a few hours' time. It temporarily rights the universe when the good guy wins and the bad guy pays.

But in real life "resolution" is really incomplete and ongoing, rather than absolute. Happily ever after is unrealistic. For example, we leave a wedding at a point of hope and happiness, that will inevitably be followed by more conflict. The part of that couple's story that we share at that moment is one resolution on a journey that is full of plot twists and more moments of resolution. None of us will live happily ever after.

In the same way, none of us will live heroically ever after either. Ultimately life doesn't tie up neatly, and people are not so easily categorized. We play the villain or the hero based on how we are motivated, and whether we choose to act on those motivations. Letting go of old habits and old motivations can be disorienting. It is comforting that God's "perfect love drives out fear" (1 John 4:18) because change, even good change, can be scary.

Christ's atonement overcomes the seven deadly sins and makes it possible for us to change. While we are supposed to participate and engage, this life is more than doing; it is being and becoming. At the heart of the Christian gospel is change that is transforming, rather than conforming. This change is not about conforming to a set of expectations, but about a journey that allows us to become more love-driven and less fear-driven. The virtues become more natural to us and the sins less satisfying as we move toward Christ.

APPENDIX

Backstory of The Seven

The seven deadly sins are never found together in the Bible as a list. There are a number of lists of sins in the Bible, and the "seven deadly sins" make individual appearances on those lists. Early church fathers like Hermas, Tertullian, and Augustine all wrote about certain sins which each considered worse than others.

Three writers in the fourth century, Evagrius, Augustine, and Cassian set the stage for how we see the seven deadly sins today. A list of "evil thoughts" may have been part of oral teachings of Egyptian monks known as "the desert fathers" for some time before they were written down by Evagrius Ponticus (345–399), a Greek serving in a monastery in Egypt. Ignoring the cool factor of the number seven, Evagrius went with eight evil thoughts which he believed inspired all evil behavior. His rankings, based on an increasing fixation with self: gluttony, lust, avarice (greed), sadness, anger, acedia (indifference), vainglory (boasting), and pride.

Around the same time Augustine was writing much of the theology that still shapes Christianity today. His contribution was to distinguish mortal sins as deliberate wrongdoing, and venial sins as accidental infractions. He defined a mortal sin as "a thought, word, or deed contrary to the eternal law... a voluntary act." It is from this Roman Catholic tradition that much of our understanding of the seven deadly sins emerges.

French ascetic John Cassian (360–435) wrote more on the subject, coining the word "vices." He created lists of sub-sins that could be categorized under each of the eight. Cassian also believed in a domino effect in which lesser sins would pave the way to more serious sins.

Sixth century Pope Gregory the Great (540–604) agreed with Cassian on this, and coined the phrase "cardinal sins." He officially reduced the list to seven. People tended to like the number seven and usually listed seven anyway, always leaving one out. He combined vainglory with pride, acedia with sadness, and added envy. His ranking, starting with the most serious, was based on how much he thought they offended love: pride, envy, anger, sadness (which didn't really catch on and was still usually called acedia), avarice, gluttony, and lust.

Pope Gregory, and later, Thomas Aquinas, were careful to distinguish "passions" (a tendency toward a particular sin) from consciously feeding these tendencies and acting upon them. Willfully entertaining the "passions" was what made them sin. Thomas Aquinas put the seven in their present form in the 13th century, and included them in his *Summa Theologica*. While Aquinas agreed with earlier theologians that the Seven would lead to other sins, he did not believe the seriousness of the sins could be ranked.

Appendix

Opposing virtues

Paul spends about half of 1 Corinthians 13 explaining what love is not, contrasting it with what love is. The chapter ends with listing three virtues: "And now these three remain: faith, hope, and love. But the greatest of these is love." Tradition names the four additional virtues: "prudence, fortitude, justice and temperance" which appear in the writings of Plato and Socrates, and in the Apocryphal *Book of Wisdom*, as well as in the New Testament.

From these sources early Christian theologians compiled the list of seven contrary virtues to oppose the seven deadly sins. Prudentius' *Psychomachia* pits each vice against a virtue. Even older lists of virtues offer variations on this list.

Greek philosopher Plato made a list which included prudence, temperance, courage, and justice. These virtues were called cardinal virtues by St. Ambrose, and the early Christian Church thought these could apply to anyone seeking to live a moral life, not only to people of faith.

Paul defined faith, hope, and love in his first letter to the Corinthians as virtues that would remain after any opportunity to perform moral deeds ends. The early church distinguished these "theological virtues" from "cardinal virtues," believing that the cardinal virtues were a reflection of moral choices while the theological virtues were a result of salvation.

Augustine reconciled the four cardinal virtues to love in this way: "Temperance is love giving itself entirely to that which is loved; fortitude is love readily bearing all things for the sake of the loved object; justice is love serving only the loved object, and therefore ruling rightly; prudence is love distinguishing with sagacity between what hinders it and what helps it."

The cardinal and theological virtues are commonly referred to as the seven virtues, while those on Prudentius' list are often called the "contrary" or "opposing" virtues because they oppose the seven deadly sins. In this book I presented opposites for each of the sins that are faithful to these virtues, but chose synonyms that better express how these virtues translate in the 21st century.

Middle ages pop culture

Throughout the Middle Ages the church designed teaching around the seven vices and the opposing virtues. A majority of people in the middle ages could not read, but those who were literate were likely to own books concerning the sins. For those who could not read, rich oral and visual traditions arose. Representative artwork was painted on church walls, and the sins were a popular subject for morality plays, which were the PBS of the middle ages.

A mythology grew up around the seven deadly sins. William Langland's *Piers Plowman*, Dante's *Divine Commedia*, Chaucer's *The Parson's Tale*, and Spenser's *Faerie Queen* are all about the seven deadly sins, and were influenced by a theologian named Peraldus.

Each sin became associated with various animals, colors, demons, and punishments in hell. We may derive expressions like "green with envy" or "seeing red" from some of these associations. In 1589 witch hunter Peter Binsfield associated demons with particular sins. The origin for the names of the demons in the following table is from various apocryphal books and other ancient myths.

Appendix

Common Middle Ages Associations with The Seven

Sin	Punishment in Hell	Animal	Color	Demon
Lust	Smothered in fire and brimstone	Cow	Blue	Asmodeus
Gluttony	Forced to eat rats, toads, and snakes	Pig	Orange	Beelzebub
Greed	Put in cauldrons of boiling oil	Frog	Yellow	Mammon
Sloth	Thrown in snake pits	Goat	Light blue	Belphegor
Anger	Dismembered alive	Bear	Red	Satan
Envy	Put in freezing water	Dog	Green	Leviathan
Pride	Broken on the wheel	Horse	Violet	Lucifer

Dante influences all of us

The most influential writer concerning the seven deadly sins was Dante. In Dante's *Inferno* souls are assigned to a ring of hell based on the sins committed while alive. Dante developed his own set of punishments. The deeper the ring, the worse the punishment, until Satan is found at the center ring. Dante included sins like heresy, blasphemy, and fraud, as well the traditional seven deadly sins. Dante further categorized the sins as stemming from either perverted love, defective love, or excessive love:

Cold Sins (perverted love) were Pride, Envy, and Anger
Sins of Improper Measure (defective love) was Sloth
Warm Sins (excessive love) were Greed, Gluttony, and Lust

Dante's Punishments:

Pride - Carrying heavy stones
Envy - Sealed eyes
Anger - Smoke
Sloth - Running
Greed - Prostration
Gluttony - Starvation
Lust - Fire

The *Inferno* popularized the idea of "rings of hell" to western culture, although this particular idea appears in the *Apocalypse of Paul* and some early Muslim works before Dante. Dante got ideas from both *The Apocalypse of Peter* and *The Apocalypse of Paul*, identified as Gnostic gospels by writers contemporary with them.

Appendix

The word "Gnostic" literally means spiritual knowledge. Gnostic gospels began showing up 100 to 300 years after the New Testament books, and are not generally accepted as gospel truth by mainstream Christian theologians. How pop culture today views the seven deadly sins and also hell and purgatory is greatly influenced by Dante's work. Those seeking a strictly biblical understanding of hell will not find scriptures about it all in one place.

In Dante's *Purgatorio* those with the possibility of redemption are assigned particular tasks to perform. He believed that purgatory was a place where sins were purged by cathartic pain. Purgatory is unique to Roman Catholic theology, though ideas like reincarnation and karma echo the concept of "just desserts" for souls that may be redeemable but are still struggling with evil motives or behaviors.

Botticelli drew this map of hell based on Dante's Inferno:

Sinema7

In the fifteenth century artist Hieronymus Bosch created a work of art representing the seven deadly sins. In it he depicted the sins as failings of everyday people in their everyday lives, which made his painting more accessible to the average person.

Incorporating humor and characters from fifteenth century pop culture into his drawings, Bosch seemed to have as little respect for the clergy as pop culture does today. In the panel on gluttony two obese people are being fed by a nun, while in the sloth vignette a man dozes by the fire while a nun chides him about his duty to the church:

Appendix

Go online and take a look at Jessica Hagy's humorous chart on her blog, *Indexed*, at: http://thisisindexed.com/2007/01/were-all-going-to-hell She combines sins to come up with some interesting social commentary. For example, Gluttony + Greed = The Last Donut. Bosch would have loved it.

Many writers and artists have translated the sins into their own cultural perspectives. As discussed earlier, the victims in the movie *Se7en* represent each of the seven sins to serial killer John Doe. Each of the seven deadly sins is incorporated into the movie *Bedazzled*, in which a present-day man is tempted by the Devil. Each scene in the movie *Clerks* supposedly addresses one of the sins. Megadeth's *Seven* describes each sin, and declares that they are all "deep fears that drive us, hid beneath disguises." Each of the seven books in C. S. Lewis' *Chronicles of Narnia* deals with one of the seven sins, and explores how characters struggling with each sin find redemption. There are films and documentaries of Dante's Inferno from 2006, 2008, and 2010.

The Vatican's New 7

These recently introduced sins emanate from some of the same old seven. They are just new ways the seven are manifested in our time:
Drug abuse = gluttony in a different form
Morally debatable experimentation = pride – playing God
Environmental pollution = mostly greed and some sloth
Causing poverty = usually greed
Social inequality and injustice = greed and envy
Genetic manipulation = pride - playing God
Accumulating excessive wealth = greed and envy

Sinema7

Other Religions List The Sins

Islam - Seven noxious things

Associating anything with Allah
Magic
Killing one whom Allah has declared inviolate without a just cause
Consuming the property of an orphan
Devouring usury
Turning back when the army advances
Slandering chaste women who are believers but indiscreet

Hinduism - Vices

O thou of great wisdom, everything about that from which spring wrath and lust, and fear and loss of judgment, and inclination to do (evil to others), and jealousy and malice and pride and envy, and slander and incapacity to bear the good of others, and unkindness and covetousness. These vices are regarded as very powerful foes of all creatures. Mahabharata, Santi Parva, Sec. CLXIII

Gandhi made this list of seven deadly sins

Wealth without Work
Pleasure without Conscience
Science without Humanity
Knowledge without Character
Politics without Principle
Commerce without Morality
Worship without Sacrifice

Appendix

Buddhism doesn't recognize "sins" per say but does lay out a code of ethics aimed at stopping suffering:

I undertake the rule to refrain from destroying living creatures.
I undertake the rule to refrain from taking that which is not given.
I undertake the rule to refrain from sexual misconduct.
I undertake the rule to refrain from incorrect speech.
I undertake the rule to refrain from intoxicants which lead to carelessness.

Ten Fetters that tie one to suffering

1. Belief in an individual self (Pali: *sakkāya-ditthi*)
2. Doubt or uncertainty, especially about the teachings (*vicikicchā*)
3. Attachment to rites and rituals (*sīlabbata-parāmāso*)
4. Sensual desire (*kāmacchando*)
5. Ill will (*vyāpādo* or *byāpādo*)
6. Lust for material existence, lust for material rebirth (*rūparāgo*)
7. Lust for immaterial existence (*arūparāgo*)
8. Pride in self, conceit, arrogance (*māno*)
9. Restlessness, distraction (*uddhaccaŋ*)
10. Ignorance (*avijja*)

THE SEVENS

7 Biblical Lists of Sins

For from within, out of a person's heart, come evil thoughts, sexual immorality, theft, murder, adultery, greed, wickedness, deceit, eagerness for lustful pleasure, envy, slander, pride, and foolishness. (Mark 7:20-22).

There are six things the Lord hates, seven that are detestable to him: haughty eyes, a lying tongue, hands that shed innocent blood, a heart that devises wicked schemes, feet that are quick to rush into evil, a false witness who pours out lies, and a man who stirs up dissension among brothers. (Proverbs 6:16-19 NIV).

When you follow the desires of your sinful nature your lives will produce these evil results: sexual immorality, impure thoughts, eagerness for lustful pleasure, idolatry, participation in demonic activities, hostility, quarreling, jealousy, outbursts of anger, selfish ambition, divisions, the feeling that everyone is wrong except those in your own little group, envy, drunkenness, wild parties, and other kinds of sin. (Gal. 5:19-21a)

And you won't spend the rest of your life chasing after evil desires, but you will be anxious to do the will of God. You have had enough in the past of the evil things that godless people enjoy - their immorality and lust, their feasting and drunkenness and wild parties... (I Peter 4:2-3)

Appendix

Whenever there is jealousy and selfish ambition, there you will find disorder and every kind of evil. (James 3:16)

But the world offers only the lust for physical pleasure, the lust for everything we see, and pride in our possessions. (1 John 2:16)

The Ten Commandments summarized (Exodus 20:1-17)

1. You shall not worship any other god but me (God, YHWH, Jehovah of Bible)
2. You shall not make a graven image
3. You shall not take the name of God in vain
4. You shall not break the Sabbath
5. You shall not dishonor your parents
6. You shall not murder
7. You shall not commit adultery
8. You shall not steal
9. You shall not commit perjury
10. You shall not covet

7 Biblical Lists of Virtues

Love is patient and kind; love does not envy or boast; it is not arrogant or rude. It does not insist on its own way; it is not irritable or resentful; it does not rejoice at wrongdoing, but rejoices with the truth. Love bears all things, believes all things, hopes all things, endures all things... There are three things that will endure, faith, hope and love – and the greatest of these is love. (1 Corinthians 13: 4-7 & 13)

When the Holy Spirit controls our lives, he will produce this kind of fruit in us: love, joy, peace, patience, kindness, goodness, faithfulness, gentleness and self-control. (Galatians 5:22)

Stand your ground, putting on the belt of truth; the body armor of God's righteousness. For shoes put on the peace that comes from the Good News... faith as your shield... salvation as your helmet; take the sword of the Spirit, which is the Word of God. (Eph. 6:14-17)

Since God chose you to be the holy people he loves, you must clothe yourselves with tenderhearted mercy, kindness, humility, gentleness, and patience. (Col. 3:12)

But the wisdom that comes from heaven is first of all pure. It is also peace loving, gentle at all times, and willing to yield to others. It is full of mercy and good deeds. It shows no partiality and is always sincere. (James 3:17)

In view of all this, make every effort to respond to God's promises. Supplement your faith with a generous provision of moral excellence, and moral excellence with knowledge, and knowledge with self-control, and self-control with patient endurance, and patient endurance with godliness, and godliness with brotherly affection, and brotherly affection with love for everyone. The more you grow like this, the more productive and useful you will be in your knowledge of our Lord Jesus Christ. (2 Peter 1:5-8)

Appendix

The Beatitudes (Matthew 5:3-11)

Blessed are:	Result:
Those who realize their need for God	They will receive the Kingdom of Heaven
Those who mourn	They will be comforted
Those who are gentle and lowly	The whole earth will belong to them
Those who seek justice	They will receive it
Those who are merciful	They will receive mercy
Those whose hearts are pure	They will see God
Those who work for peace	They will be called God's children
Those who are persecuted for God's sake	They will receive the Kingdom of God

7 Scriptures About Each of The Seven

Lust

Run from anything that stimulates youthful lusts. Instead, pursue righteous living... (2 Tim. 2:22)

Run from sexual sin! No other sin so clearly affects the body as this one does. For sexual immorality is a sin against your own body. (I Cor. 6:18)

Don't lust for her beauty. Don't let her coy glances seduce you. For a prostitute will bring you to poverty, but sleeping with another man's wife will cost you your life. (Prov. 6:25-26)

Since you have heard about Jesus and have learned the truth that comes from him, throw off your old sinful nature and your former way of life, which is corrupted by lust and deception. (Eph. 4:21-22)

Do not let any part of your body become an instrument of evil to serve sin. Instead, give yourselves completely to God, for you were dead, but now you have new life. So use your whole body as an instrument to do what is right for the glory of God. (Rom. 6:13)

Temptation comes from our own desires, which entice us and drag us away. These desires give birth to sinful actions. And when sin is allowed to grow, it gives birth to death. (James 1:14-15)

But I say, anyone who even looks at a woman with lust has already committed adultery with her in his heart. (Matt. 5:28)

Gluttony

Do not carouse with drunkards or feast with gluttons, for they are on their way to poverty, and too much sleep clothes them in rags. (Prov. 23:20-21)

Wine produces mockers; alcohol leads to brawls. Those led astray by drink cannot be wise. (Prov. 20:1)

Appendix

While dining with a ruler, pay attention to what is put before you. If you are a big eater, put a knife to your throat. (Proverbs 23:1-2)

Sodom's sins were pride, gluttony, and laziness, while the poor and needy suffered outside her door. (Ezekiel 16:49)

When the Holy Spirit controls our lives, he will produce this kind of fruit in us: love, joy, peace, patience, kindness, goodness, faithfulness, gentleness, and self-control. Here there is no conflict with the law. (Gal. 5:22-23)

Happy is the land whose king is a noble leader and whose leaders feast at the proper time to gain strength for their work, not to get drunk. (Ecc. 10:17)

So go ahead. Eat your food with joy, and drink your wine with a happy heart, for God approves of this. (Ecc. 9:7)

Greed

Don't store up treasures here on earth, where moths eat them and rust destroys them, and where thieves break in and steal. (Matt. 6:19)

But people who long to be rich fall into temptation and are trapped by many foolish and harmful desires that plunge them into ruin and destruction. For the love of money is the root of all kinds of evil. And some people, craving money, have wandered from the true faith and pierced themselves with many sorrows. (1 Tim. 6:9-10)

So you cannot become my disciple without giving up everything you own. (Luke 14:33)

Your gold and silver have become worthless. The very wealth you were counting on will eat away your flesh like fire. This treasure you have accumulated will stand as evidence against you on the Day of Judgment. (James 5:3)

You can be sure that no immoral, impure, or greedy person will inherit the Kingdom of Christ and of God. For a greedy person is an idolater, worshiping the things of this world. (Eph. 5:5)

For they oppressed the poor and left them destitute. They foreclosed on their homes. They were always greedy and never satisfied. Nothing remains of all the things they dreamed about. (Job 20:19-20)

But these people set an ambush for themselves; they are trying to get themselves killed. Such is the fate of all who are greedy for money; it robs them of life. (Prov. 1:18-19)

Sloth

What counts is whether we have been transformed into a new creation. (Gal. 6:15b)

Yet what we suffer now is nothing compared to the glory he will reveal to us later. (Rom. 8:18)

Lazy people irritate their employers, like vinegar to the teeth or smoke in the eyes. (Prov. 10:26)

Work hard and become a leader; be lazy and become a slave. (Prov. 12:24)

Never be lazy, but work hard and serve the Lord enthusiastically. (Rom. 12:11)

Then you will not become spiritually dull and indifferent. Instead, you will follow the example of those who are going to inherit God's promises because of their faith and endurance. (Heb. 6:12)

Remember, it is sin to know what you ought to do and then not do it. (James 4:17)

Anger

A gentle answer turns away wrath, but a harsh word stirs up anger. (Prov. 15:1 NIV)

Fools vent their anger, but the wise quietly hold it back. (Prov. 29:11)

Stop being angry! Turn from your rage! Do not lose your temper – it only leads to harm. (Ps. 37:8)

And don't sin by letting anger control you. Don't let the sun go down while you are still angry, for anger gives a foothold to the devil. (Eph. 4:26-27)

Get rid of all bitterness, rage, anger, harsh words, and slander, as well as all types of evil behavior. (Eph. 4:31)

In every place of worship, I want men to pray with holy hands lifted up to God, free from anger and controversy. (I Tim. 2:8)

Understand this my dear brothers and sisters: you must all be quick to listen, slow to speak, and slow to get angry. (James 1:19)

Envy

Anger is cruel and fury overwhelming, but who can stand before jealousy. (Prov. 27:4 NIV)

Surely resentment destroys the fool, and jealousy kills the simple. (Job 5:2)

Then I observed that most people are motivated to success because they envy their neighbors. But this, too, is meaningless - like chasing the wind. (Ecc. 4:4)

So don't be dismayed when the wicked grow rich and their homes become ever more splendid. (Ps. 49:16)

For he realized by now that the leading priests had arrested Jesus out of envy. (Mark 15:10)

So get rid of all evil behavior. Be done with all deceit, hypocrisy, jealousy, and all unkind speech. (I Pet. 2:1)

No lusting after your neighbor's house - or wife or servant or maid or ox or donkey. Don't set your heart on anything that is your neighbor's. (Ex. 20:17 Message)

Appendix

Pride

They scoff and speak only evil; in their pride they seek to crush others. (Ps. 73:8)

Pride goes before destruction, and haughtiness before a fall. (Prov. 16:18)

Pride ends in humiliation, while humility brings honor. (Prov. 29:23)

Human pride will be humbled, and human arrogance will be brought down. (Is. 2:17a)

You have been deceived by your own pride because you live in a rock fortress and make your home high in the mountains. 'Who can ever reach us way up here?" you ask boastfully. (Obadiah 1:3)

But I will come - and soon - if the Lord lets me, and then I'll find out whether these arrogant people just give pretentious speeches or whether they really have God's power. (I Cor. 4:19)

For all that is in the world - the lust of the flesh, the lust of the eyes, and the pride of life - is not of the Father but is of the world. (1 John 2:16 NKJV)

Sinema7

Movies About All 7 Deadly Sins

Se7en (1995)
Bedazzled (1967)
Bedazzled (2000)
Clerks (1994)
Seven Deadly Sins (1993)
The Seven Deadly Sins (1962)
The Magnificent Seven Deadly Sins (1971)

Lustful Marquee

Unfaithful
Indecent Proposal
Weird Science
Fatal Attraction
American Beauty
How Stella got her Groove Back
Moonstruck

Gluttonous Marquee

Heavyweights
Ratatouille
Charlie and the Chocolate Factory
Chocolat
What's Eating Gilbert Grape
Leaving Las Vegas
Traffic

Appendix

Greedy Marquee

Wall Street
Three Kings
Oceans Eleven
Fargo
No Country For Old Men
Millions
Blood Diamond

Slothful Marquee

Slacker
The Big Liebowski
Billy Madison
Office Space
Camp Nowhere
Failure to Launch
Shaun of the Dead

Angry Marquee

Unforgiven
Crash
Falling Down
Pulp Fiction
Fight Club
V for Vendetta
The Usual Suspects

Sinema7

Envious Marquee

Toy Story
The Lion King
Gladiator
Amadeus
Single White Female
Drop Dead Gorgeous
Othello

Prideful Marquee

Batman: The Dark Knight
The Devil Wears Prada
The Mission
Die Hard
Pride and Prejudice
Harry Potter and the Order of the Phoenix
Jesus of Montreal

Appendix

Songs About All 7 Deadly Sins

It's a Sin - Pet Shop Boys
Seventh Son of a Seventh Son - Iron Maiden
7 Deadly Sins - Simple Minds
Seven - Megadeth
Bank of Bad Habits - Jimmy Buffet
Seven Deadly Sins - Traveling Wilburys
Heaven and Hell - Joe Jackson

Lustful Playlist

College Girls are Easy – Eazy E
Girls, Girls, Girls – Motley Crue
Hot for Teacher – Van Halen
Black Dog – Led Zeppelin
Let's Get it On – Marvin Gaye
Sex Machine – James Brown
Ragdoll – Aerosmith

Gluttonous Playlist

Cocaine – Eric Clapton
I Want Candy – Bow Wow Wow
Mr. Brownstone – Guns 'n' Roses
Dr. Feelgood – Motley Crue
Fat Bottomed Girls – Queen
Whiskey River – Willie Nelson
Wrong Way – Sublime

Sinema7

Greedy Playlist

Money – Pink Floyd
Material Girl – Madonna
Snakecharmer – Rage Against the Machine
Union Sundown – Bob Dylan
Mountain of Things – Tracey Chapman
Fistful of Diamonds – Wasp
Johnny the Fox Meets Jimmy the Weed – Thin Lizzy

Slothful Playlist

I Want to Be Sedated – Ramones
Because I Got High – Afroman
Comfortably Numb – Pink Floyd
Sittin' on the Dock of the Bay – Otis Redding
I'm Bored – Iggy Pop
Banana Pancakes – Jack Johnson
I'm Only Sleeping - Beatles

Angry Playlist

Fooling Yourself – Styx
You Oughta Know – Alanis Morissette
Let the Bodies Hit the Floor – Drowning Pool
Song For The Dumped – Ben Folds Five
Seek and Destroy – Metallica
The One I Love – REM
Since U Been Gone – Kelly Clarkson

Appendix

Envious Playlist

Jessie's Girl – Rick Springfield
Girlfriend – Avril Lavigne
What's Your Name – Lynyrd Skynyrd
Die, Die, My Darling – Misfits
Just My Imagination – Temptations
Professional Jealousy – Van Morrison
Chump – Green Day

Prideful Playlist

Baby I'm a Star – Prince
World's Greatest – R. Kelly
P.I.M.P. – 50 Cent
Forgot About Dre – Dr. Dre
Talkin' About Me – Toby Keith
You're So Vain – Carly Simon
Desperado - Eagles

BIBLIOGRAPHY

Introduction

Eszterhas, Joe. *Basic Instinct*. Dir. Paul Verhoeven. Carolco Pictures, 1992.

Harris, Thomas (novel); Ted Tally (screenplay). *Silence of the Lambs*. Dir. Jonathan Demme. Orion Pictures, 1991.

Holy Bible. New Living Translation. Carol Stream, IL Tyndale, 1996.

Lewis, C. S. Quoted in Paul Holmer. *C. S. Lewis: The Shape of his faith and thought*. Harper, 1976.

Smith, Dodie (novel); Bill Peet (story). *101 Dalmatians*. Dir. Clyde Geronimi, Hamilton S. Luske, and Wolfgang Reitherman. Walt Disney, 1961.

Weiser, Stanley and Oliver Stone. *Wall Street*. Dir. Oliver Stone. Twentieth Century Fox, 1987.

Lust

Allen, Woody. *Deconstructing Harry*. Dir. Woody Allen. Jean Doumanian Productions, 1997.

Anderson, Paul Thomas. *Boogie Nights*. Dir. Paul Thomas Anderson. New Line, 1997.

Bibliography

Apatow, Judd & Steve Carell. *The 40-Year Old Virgin*. Dir. Judd Apatow. Universal Pictures, 2005.

Bach, Danilo (story); Daniel Petrie, Jr. (screenplay). *Beverly Hills Cop*. Dir. Martin Brest. Paramount, 1984.

Ball, Alan. *American Beauty*. Dir. Sam Mendes. Dreamworks, 1999.

Bergman, Andrew. *The In-Laws*. Dir. Arthur Hiller. Warner Bros, 1979.

Brashares, Ann (novel); Delia Ephron. *The Sisterhood of the Travelling Pants*. Dir. Ken Kwapis. Alcon Entertainment, 2005.

Coppola, Sofia. *Lost in Translation*. Dir. Sofia Coppola. Focus Features, 2003.

Crowe, Cameron. *Jerry Maguire*. Dir. Cameron Crowe. Gracie Films, 1996.

Curtis, Richard. *Love Actually*. Dir. Richard Curtis. Universal, 2003.

Davlin, Dean and Roland Emmerich. *Independence Day*. Dir. Roland Emmerich. Centropolis Entertainment, 1996.

Eco, Umberto (novel); Andrew Birken (screenplay). *The Name of the Rose*. Dir. Jean-Jacques Bernard. Neue Constantin Films, 1986.

Elfont, Harry and Deborah Kaplan. *Can't Hardly Wait*. Columbia Pictures, 1998.

Ephron, Nora. *When Harry Met Sally*. Dir. Rob Reiner. Castle Rock Entertainment, 1989.

Finder, Joseph (story); Yuri Zeltzer (screenplay). *High Crimes*. Dir. Carl Franklin. Regency Entertainment, 2002.

Garcia, Eric (book); Nicholas Griffin (screenplay). *Matchstick Men*. Dir. Ridley Scott. Warner Brothers, 2003.

Goldman, William. *The Princess Bride*. Dir Rob Reiner. Act III Company, 1987.

Harris, Timothy & Herschel Weingrod. *Trading Places*. Dir. John Landis. Cinema Group Ventures, 1983.

Herlihy, Tim. *The Wedding Singer*. Dir. Frank Coraci. Juno Pix, 1998.

Herz, Adam. *American Pie*. Dir. Paul Weitz. Universal, 1999.

Holy Bible. New Living Translation. Carol Stream, IL Tyndale, 1996.

Lancaster, Bill and Glenn Ficarra. *Bad News Bears*. Dir. Richard Linklater. Detour Filmproduction, 2005.

Lawton, J. F. *Pretty Woman*. Dir. Garry Marshall. Touchstone Pictures, 1990.

Leven, Jeremy and Lord Byron. *Don Juan de Marco*. Dir. Jeremy Levin. New Line Cinema, 1994.

Luhrmann, Baz and Craig Pearce. *Moulin Rouge*. Dir. Baz Luhrmann. Bazmark Films, 2001.

Naughton, Lewis. *Alfie*. Dir. Lewis Gilbert. Lewis Gilbert, 1966.

O'Brein, John (novel), Mike Figgis (screenplay). *Leaving Las Vegas*. Dir. Mike Figgis. Initial Productions, 1995.

Rogen, Seth and Evan Goldberg. *Superbad*. Dir. Greg Mottola. Columbia, 2007.

Ross, Gary. *Pleasantville*. Dir. Gary Ross. New Line Cinema, 1998.

Sparks, Nicholas (novel); Karen Janszen (screenplay). *A Walk to Remember*. Dir. Adam Shankman. DiNovi Pictures, 2002.

Stanley, John Patrick. *Moonstruck*. Dir. Norman Jewison. Metro-Goldwyn-Mayer, 1987.

Westermann, John (novel); Ed Horowitz (screenplay). *Exit Wounds*. Dir. Andrzej Bartkowiak. Village Roadshow, 2001.

Gluttony

Apatow, Judd & Steven Brill. *Heavy Weights*. Dir. Steven Brill. Caravan Pictures, 1995.

Aquinas, Thomas. *Summa Theologica of Saint Thomas Aquinas*. Second and Revised Edition, 1920. Online edition. New Advent. 28 Dec 2006 http://www.newadvent.org/summa/2084.htm

Bird, Brad, Jan Pinkava, and Jim Capobianco. *Ratatouille*. Dir. Brad Bird and Jan Pinkava. Pixar, 2007.

Brooks, Mel. *History of the World Part I*. Dir. Mel Brooks. Brooksfilms, 1981.

Buckley, Christopher (novel); Jason Reitman (screenplay). *Thank You for Smoking*. Dir. Jason Reitman. Room 9 Entertainment, 2005.

Chapman, Graham, John Cleese, Terry Gilliam, Eric Idle, Terry Jones, Michael Palin. *The Meaning of Life*. Dir. Terry Jones & Terry Gilliam. Celandine Films, 1983.

Cooney, Joan Ganz (creator). *Sesame Street*. TV Series, 1969-2008.

Foote, Horton. *Tender Mercies*. Dir. Bruce Beresford. Antron Media Production, 1983.

Grant, Susannah. *28 Days*. Dir. Betty Thomas. Columbia, 2000.

Bibliography

Groening, Matt (creator). *The Simpsons / Homer's Odyssey*. Season 1 Episode 3. Fox 21, Jan 1990.

Harris, Joanne (novel); Robert Nelson Jacobs (screenplay). *Chocolat*. Dir. Lasse Hallström. Miramax Films, 2000.

Hedges, Peter. *What's Eating Gilbert Grape*. Dir. Lasse Halstrom. J & M Entertainment, 1993.

Holy Bible. New Living Translation. Carol Stream, IL Tyndale, 1996.

Johnson, Randall and Oliver Stone. *The Doors*. Dir. Oliver Stone. Bill Graham Films, 1991.

Moore, Simon (miniseries); Stephen Gaghan (screenplay). *Traffic*. Dir. Steven Soderbergh. Bedford Falls Productions, 2001.

Myers, Mike and Michael McCullers. *Austin Powers: The Spy Who Shagged Me*. Dir. Jay Roach. New Line Cinema, 1999.

O'Brein, John (novel); Mike Figgis (screenplay). *Leaving Las Vegas*. Dir. Mike Figgis. Initial Productions, 1995.

Peterson, Eugene. *The Message: The Bible in Contemporary Language*. NavPress, 2007.

Pickett, Rex (novel); Alexander Payne and Jim Taylor (screenplay). *Sideways*. Dir. Alexander Payne. Fox Searchlight, 2005.

Pizzo, Angelo. *Rudy*. Dir. David Anspaugh. TriStar Pictures, 1993.

Ramis, Harold, Douglas Kenny, and Chris Miller. *Animal House*. Dir. John Landis. Universal Pictures, 1978.

Spurlock, Morgan. *Supersize Me*. Dir. Morgan Spurlock. Kathbur Pictures, 2004.

Greed

Bell, Elsa and Bob Ducsay (story); Elsa Bell (screenplay). *Vegas Vacation*. Dir. Stephen Kessler. Warner Bros., 1997.

Blixen, Karen & Gabriel Axel. *Babette's Feast*. Dir. Gabriel Axel. Panorama Films, 1987.

Boesky, Ivan. *Commencement Address*, School of Business Administration, University of California. 18 May 1986.

Boyce, Frank Cottrell. *Millions*. Dir. Danny Boyle. Pathe Pictures International, 2004.

Coen, Joel & Ethan. *Fargo*. Dir. Joel & Ethan Coen. Polygram Filmed Entertainment, 1996.

Cribs. Prod. MTV Productions. 2000-2007.

Dickens, Charles (novel); Noel Langley (story). *Scrooge*. Dir. Brian Desmond Hurst. George Minter Productions, 1951.

Bibliography

Elliot, Ted & Terry Rossio. *Pirates of the Caribbean: The Curse of the Black Pearl*. Dir. Gore Verbinski. Walt Disney Pictures, 2003.

Crowe, Cameron. *Jerry Maguire*. Dir. Cameron Crowe. Gracie Films, 1996.

Goodrich, Frances, Albert Hackett, & Frank Capra. *It's a Wonderful Life*. Dir. Frank Capra. Liberty Films, 1946.

Griffin, Ted (screenplay). *Oceans Eleven*. Dir. Stephen Soderbergh. Warner, 2001.

Harris, Timothy and Herschel Weingrod. *Trading Places*. Dir. John Landis. Cinema Group Ventures, 1983.

Holy Bible. New Living Translation. Carol Stream, IL Tyndale, 1996.

Homer (Poem); David Benioff (screenplay). *Troy*. Dir. Wolfgang Petersen. Warner Bros., 2004.

Hyde, Catherine Ryan & Leslie Dixon. *Pay It Forward*. Dir. Mimi Leder. Warner Brothers, 2000.

Jay Leno: Delivering Hope and Laughter. Positive Magazine, April 2008 p. 20. http://issuu.com/positivemagazine/docs/april2008?mode=embed&documentId=080506184952-b79f220a91a74960b2ab29fbfc1b3c03&layout=grey

Leavitt, Charles & C. Gaby Mitchell (story); Charles Leavitt (screenplay). *Blood Diamond*. Dir. Edward Zwick. Warner Brothers, 2006.

Lederer, Charles (screenplay); Joseph Fields (musical comedy). *Gentlemen Prefer Blondes*. Dir. Howard Hawks. Twentieth Century Fox, 2001.

Loy, David. *Shall We Pave the Planet or Learn to Wear Shoes: A Buddhist Perspective on Greed and Globalization*. Bunkyo University, Japan. 18 Aug 2009 http://www.bpf.org/tsangha/loy-globo.html

Mad Magazine. D.C. Comics http://www.dccomics.com/mad/ quoted by Rebecca Sato in *The Consumer Paradox: Scientists Find that Low Self-Esteem and Materialism goes Hand in Hand*. Nov. 13, 2007. *The Daily Galaxy*. 14 Feb. 2009. http://www.dailygalaxy.com/my_weblog/2007/11/the-consumer-pa.html

Martin, Steve and Carl Gottlieb (story); Steve Martin, Carl Gottlieb, & Michael Elias (screenplay). *The Jerk*. Dir. Carl Reiner. Aspen Film Society, 1979.

McFarlane, Seth (creator); Mike Barker and Matt Weitzman (writers). *Family Guy / Peter Griffin: Husband, Father... Brother?* Dir. Scott Wood. Season 3 Episode 14. Cartoon Network. Orig. air date 6 Dec 2001.

McCarthy, Cormac (novel); Joel & Ethan Coen (screenplay). *No Country for Old Men*. Dir. Joel & Ethan Coen. Paramount Vantage, 2009.

Bibliography

Morrow, Barry (story); Ronald Bass & Barry Morrow (screenplay). *Rain Man*. Dir. Barry Levinson. United Artists, 1988.

Palahniuk, Chuck (novel); Jim Uhls (screenplay). *Fight Club*. Dir David Fincher. Art Linson Productions, 1999.

Russell, David O. & Jeff Baena. *I Heart Huckabee's*. Dir. David O. Russell. Searchlight Productions, 2004.

Tickle, Phyllis. *Greed: The Mother of All Sins*. Beliefnet. July, 2002. 14 Nov. 2007 http://www.beliefnet.com/Faiths/2002/07/Greed-The-Mother-Of-All-Sins.aspx?p=2

Tolkein, J. R. R. (novel); Fran Walsh, Phillipa Boyens, Peter Jackson (screenplay). *The Lord of the Rings*. Dir. Peter Jackson. New Line, 2001-2003.

Trail, Armitage (novel); Olive Stone, Ben Hecht, and Howard Hawks (screenplay). *Scarface*. Dir. Brian DePalma. Universal Pictures, 1983.

Weiser, Stanley and Oliver Stone. *Wall Street*. Dir. Oliver Stone. Twentieth Century Fox, 1987.

Sloth

Adams, Douglas. *A Hitchhiker's Guide to the Galaxy*. Dir. Garth Jennings. Touchstone Pictures, 2005.

Aquinas, Thomas. *Summa Theologica*. Question 84. http://www.newadvent.org/summa/2084.htm

Astle, Tom J. and Matt Ember. *Failure to Launch*. Dir. Tom Dey. Paramount Pictures, 2006.

Brooks, Mel and Thomas Meehan. *Spaceballs*. Dir. Mel Brooks. Brooksfilms, 1987.

Castle, Nick and James V. Hart. *August Rush*. Dir. Kirsten Sheridan. C. J. Entertainment, 2007.

Chayefsky, Paddy. *Network*. Dir. Sidney Lumet. MGM, 1976.

Coen, Ethan and Joel. *The Big Lebowski*. Dir. Joel Coen. Polygram Filmed Entertainment, 1998.

Csikszentmihalyi, Mihaly. *Flow: the Psychology of Optimal Experience*. Harper, 1991.

Herilhy, Tim and Adam Sandler. *Billy Madison*. Dir. Tamra Davis. Universal, 1995.

Dante Aligheiri. *The Inferno of Dante*. Tr. Robert Pinsky. Farrar, Straus and Giroux, 1997.

Ebert, George. "Conversations in Management: Douglas Adams." *EzineArticles* 23 November 2005. 09 February 2008 http://ezinearticles.com/?Conversations-in-Management:-Douglas-Adams&id=101442

Evagrius Ponticus: Various introductory texts on Virtues and Vices. Fr. Luke Dysinger, St. Andrew's Abbey, 1990. http://www.ldysinger.com/Evagrius/00a_start.htm

Bibliography

Groening, Matt (creator). *The Simpsons /Monty Can't Buy Me Love*. Season 10 Episode 21. Fox. 2 Dec 1999.

Mitch Hedberg on MySpace. Web. 12 Oct. 2008. http://www.myspace.com/mitchhedbergmix

Holy Bible. New Living Translation. Carol Stream, IL Tyndale, 1996.

Hughes, John. *Ferris Bueller's Day Off*. Dir. John Hughes. Paramount, 1986.

Hughes, John. *Uncle Buck*. Hughes Entertainment, 1989.

Kurtzman, Andrew and Eliot Wald. *Camp Nowhere*. Dir. Jonathan Prince. Hollywood Pictures, 1994.

Judge, Mike. *Office Space*. Dir. Mike Judge. Twentieth Century Fox Corporation, 1999.

Lennon, John and Paul McCartney. *I'm Only Sleeping. Revolver*. Capitol, 1966.

Linklater, Richard. *Slacker*. Dir. Richard Linklater. Detour Filmproduction, 1991.

Lucas, George (story); Leigh Brackett and Lawrence Kasdan (screenplay). *Star Wars: The Empire Strikes Back*. Dir. Ivan Kershner. Lucasfilm, 1980.

Myers, Mike. *Austin Powers: International Man of Mystery*. Dir. Jay Roach. Capella International, 1997.

Rubin, Danny and Harold Ramis. *Groundhog Day*. Dir. Harold Ramis. Columbia Pictures, 1993.

Sayers, Dorothy. "The Other Six Deadly Sins." *The Whimsical Christian*. Collier Books, 1987.

Shyamalan, M. Night. *Lady in the Water*. Dir. M. Night Shyamalan. Warner Bros., 2006.

Spottiswoode, Roger, et al. *48 Hours*. Dir. Walter Hill. Paramount Pictures, 1982.

Weisberg, David, Douglas Cook, and Mark Rosner. *The Rock*. Hollywood Pictures, 1996.

Welland, Colin. *Chariots of Fire*. Dir. Hugh Hudson. Enigma Productions, 1981.

Wilson, Michael J. (story); Michael Berg (screenplay). *Ice Age*. Chris Wedge and Carlos Saldanha. Blue Sky Studios, 2002.

Anger

Damon, Matt and Ben Affleck. *Good Will Hunting*. Dir. Gus Van Sant. Be Gentlemen Ltd. Partnership, 1997.

Dubus, Andre (novel); Vadim Perelman (screenplay). *The House of Sand and Fog*. Dir. Vadim Perelman. Dreamworks, 2003.

Holy Bible. New Living Translation. Carol Stream, IL Tyndale, 1996.

Bibliography

Keneally, Thomas and Stephen Zaillian. *Schindler's List.* Dir. Stephen Spielberg. Universal Pictures, 1993.

Kuschner, Tony and Eric Roth. *Munich.* Dir. Steven Spielberg. Dreamworks, SKG, 2005.

Mamet, David. *Glengarry Glen Ross.* Dir. Mike Nichols. GGR, 1992.

Neibuhr, Reinhold. *The Serenity Prayer.* Bartlett's Familiar Quotations, 16th edn., ed. Justin Kaplan, 1992, p. 684

Palahniuk, Chuck (novel); Jim Uhls (screenplay). *Fight Club.* Dir David Fincher. Art Linson Productions, 1999.

Pearson, Keir and Terry George. *Hotel Rwanda.* Dir. Terry George. United Artists, 2004.

Peoples, David Webb. *Unforgiven.* Dir. Clint Eastwood. Malpaso Productions, 1992.

Schur, Michael, B. J. Novak, Paul Lieberstein, and Mindy Kaling. *The Office.* Prod. Greg Daniels. Cr. Ricky Gervais. NBC, 2005 - .

Smith, Ebbie Roe. *Falling Down.* Dir. Joel Schumacher. Alcor Films, 1993.

Tarantino, Quentin and Roger Avary. *Pulp Fiction.* Dir. Quentin Tarantino. A Band Apart, 1994.

Tolkein, J.R.R. (novel); Walsh, Fran (screenplay) *The Lord of the Rings.* Dir. Peter Jackson. New Line, 2001-2003.

Wade, Kevin. *Working Girl*. Dir. Mike Nichols. Twentieth Century Fox, 1988.

Walker, Andrew Kevin. *Se7en*. Dir. David Fincher. New Line Cinema, 1995.

Weiss, Marie (story); Richard Gravenese (screenplay). *The Ref.* Dir. Ted. Demme. Don Simpson/Jerry Bruckheimer Films, 1994.

Wiseman, Rosalind (book); Tina Fey (screenplay). *Mean Girls*. Dir. Mark Waters. Paramount Pictures, 2004.

Wiseman, Rosalind. *Queen Bees and Wannabes: Helping Your Daughter Survive Cliques, Gossip, Boyfriends, and Other Realities of Adolescence.* Three Rivers Press, 2003

Envy

Andrus, Mark (story); Mark Andrus and James Brooks (screenplay). *As Good as It Gets*. Dir. James Brooks. TriStar, 1997.

Aristotle. *Rhetoric*. Book II Ch. 10 http://www.public.iastate.edu/~honeyl/Rhetoric/rhet2-10.html

Crowe, Cameron. *Elizabethtown*. Dir. Cameron Crowe. Paramount, 2005.

Ferguson, James, Robert Shallcross, Tommy Swerdlow, Michael Goldberg. *Little Giants*. Dir. Duane Dunham. Warner, 1994.

Bibliography

Guest, Christopher and Michael McKean. *This is Spinal Tap*. Dir. Rob Reiner. Spinal Tap Productions, 1984.

Groom, Winston (novel); Eric Roth (screenplay). *Forrest Gump*. Dir. Robert Zemeckis. Paramount, 1994.

Holy Bible. New Living Translation. Carol Stream, IL Tyndale, 1996.

Hornby, Nick (book); D. V. DeVincentis (screenplay). *High Fidelity*. Dir. Stephen Frears. Dogstar Films, 2000.

Jeffreys, Stephen. *The Libertine*. Dir. Laurence Dunmore. The Weinstein Company, 2004.

Lasseter, John, Pete Docter, Andrew Stanton, Joe Ranft. *Toy Story*. Dir. John Lasseter. Disney, 1995.

Mecchi, Irene, Jonathan Roberts, Linda Woolverton. *The Lion King*. Dir. Robert Allers and Rob Minkoff. Disney, 1994.

Rubin, Bruce Joel and Michael Tolkin. *Deep Impact*. Dir. Mimi Leder. Paramount, 1998.

Rueff, Roger. *The Big Kahuna*. Dir. John Swanbeck. Franchise Pictures, 1999.

Rostand, Edmund (play); Steve Martin (screenplay). *Roxanne*. Dir. Fred Schepisi. Columbia Pictures Corp., 1987.

Shaffer, Peter. *Amadeus*. Dir. Milos Forman. The Saul Zaentz Company, 1984.
(In fairness to the real Salieri, the story is based on an Alexander Pushkin poem written in 1830 which Shaffer used as inspiration for his screenplay. The real Salieri was apparently a successful family man who was respected as a musician and even taught music to Mozart's son.)

Sinclair, Upton (novel); Paul Thomas Anderson. *There Will Be Blood*. Dir. Paul Thomas Anderson. Goulardi Film Company, 2007.

Tolkein, J.R.R. (novel); Walsh, Fran (screenplay) *The Lord of the Rings*. Dir. Peter Jackson. New Line, 2001-2003.

Turner, Bonnie and Terry Turner. *Tommy Boy*. Dir. Pete Segal. Paramount, 1995.

Pride

Armstrong, James. *Volcano*. Dir. Mick Jackson. Donner / Schuler-Donner / Twentieth Century Fox, 1997.

Austen, Jane (novel); Deborah Moggach (screenplay). *Pride and Prejudice*. Dir. Joe Wright. Focus Feature, 2005.

Bible. New Living Translation. Micah 6:8; Phil. 2:3-5; I Cor. 1:27

Bolt, Robert (play), Ronald Joffe (screenplay). *The Mission*. Warner Bros., 1986.

Bibliography

Bonhem, Leslie. *Dante's Peak*. Dir. Roger Donaldson. Pacific Western / MCA / Universal, 1996.

Crichton, Michael and Anne-Marie Martin. *Twister*. Dir. Jan de Bont. Warner Bros., 1996.

Crowe, Cameron. *Say Anything*. Dir. Cameron Crowe. Gracie Films, 1989.

Doyle-Murray, Brian, Harold Ramis, and Douglas Kenney. *Caddyshack*. Dir Harold Ramis. Orion Pictures, 1980.

Emmerich, Roland. *The Day After Tomorrow*. Dir. Roland Emmerich. Twentieth Century Fox, 2004.

Hensleigh, Jonathan and J. J. Abrams (screenplay). *Armageddon*. Dir. Michael Bay. Touchstone, 1998.

Holy Bible. New Living Translation. Carol Stream, IL Tyndale, 1996.

How Do I Look? Dir. Marci Klein and Renee G. Howard. TV Series. Style Network, 2004-2008.

Howard, Gregory Allen. *Remember the Titans*. Dir. Boaz Yakin. Jerry Bruckheimer Films, 2000.

Kennedy, Duncan, Donna and Wayne Powers. *Deep Blue Sea*. Dir Renny Harlin. Twentieth Century Fox, 1999.

Launer, Dale. *My Cousin Vinny*. Dir. Jonathan Lynn. Palo Vista Productions, 1992.

Lee, Stan and Steve Ditko (comic book); David Koepp (screenplay). *Spiderman*. Dir. Sam Raimi. Columbia Pictures, 2002.

Lewis, C. S. *Mere Christianity*. NY: MacMillan, 1943-1994.

Neiderman, Andrew (novel); Jonathan Lemkin and Tony Gilroy (screenplay). *The Devil's Advocate*. Warner Bros., 1997.

Nolan, Jonathan and Christopher. *Batman: The Dark Knight*. Dir. Christopher Nolan. Warner Bros., 2008.

Protosevich, Mark and Akiva Goldsman. *I am Legend*. Dir. Francis Lawrence. Warner Bros., 2007.

Puzo, Mario. *The Godfather*. Dir. Francis Ford Coppola. Alfran/Paramount, 1972.

Rubin, Bruce Joel and Michael Tolkin. *Deep Impact*. Dir. Mimi Leder. Paramount, 1998.

Shyamalan, M. Night. *The Happening*. Dir. M. Night Shyamalan. Blinding Edge Pictures, / Twentieth Century Fox, 2008.

Stanton, Andrew. *Finding Nemo*. Dir. Andrew Stanton and Lee Unkrich. Walt Disney Pictures, 2003.

Thorp, Roderick (novel); Job Stuart and Steven E. deSouza (screenplay). *Die Hard*. Dir. John McTiernan. Twentieth Century Fox, 1988.

Bibliography

Tolkein, J.R.R. (novel); Fran Walsh, Phillipa Boyens, Peter Jackson (screenplay). *The Lord of the Rings*. Dir. Peter Jackson. New Line, 2001-2003.

Weisberger, Lauren (novel); Aline Brosh McKenna (screenplay). *The Devil Wears Prada*. Dir. David Frankel. Fox 2000 Pictures, 2006.

Wachowski, Andy and Larry. *The Matrix*. Andy and Larry Wachowski. Groucho Film Partnership / Warner, 1999.

What Not to Wear. (TV Series). BBC Productions (USA), 2002-2009.

Woolverton, Linda (screenplay). *Beauty and the Beast*. Dir. Gary Trousdale and Kirk Wise. Silver Screen Partners IV and Disney, 1991.

Yonay, Ehud and Jim Cash. *Top Gun*. Dir. Tony Scott. Paramount, 1996.

Conclusion

Brooks, Mel and Thomas Meehan. *Spaceballs*. Dir. Mel Brooks. Brooksfilms, 1987.

De Saint Expuery, Antoine. Tr. Stuart Gilbert. *The Wisdom of Sands*. Univ. of Chicago Press, 1984.

Gerwirtz, Russell. *Inside Man*. Dir. Spike Lee. Universal Pictures, 2006.

Helm, Zach. *Stranger Than Fiction*. Dir Marc. Foster. Columbia Pictures, 2006.

Holy Bible. New Living Translation. Carol Stream, IL Tyndale, 1996.

Johannson, Dave and Nick Schenk (story); Nick Schenk (screenplay). *Gran Torino*. Dir. Clint Eastwood. Matten Productions, 2008.

Irving, John (novel); Mark Steven Johnson. *Simon Birch*. Dir. Mark Steven Johnson. Hollywood Pictures, 1998.

Lewis, C. S. *Miracles*. San Francisco: HarperCollins, 1947.

Linklater, Richard. *Dazed and Confused*. Dir. Richard Linklater. Alphaville Films / Criterion, 1993.

McEwan, Ian (novel); Christopher Hampton (screenplay). Atonement. Dir. Joe Wright. Universal Pictures, 2007.

Rowling, J.K. (novel); Michael Goldenberg (screenplay). *Harry Potter and the Order of the Phoenix*. Warner Bros., 2007.

Walker, Andrew Kevin. *Se7en*. Dir. David Fincher. New Line Cinema, 1995.

Wachowski, Andy and Larry. *V for Vendetta*. Dir. James McTeigue. Silver Pictures / Warner Bros, 2005.

Ziskin, Laura, Alvin Sargent, and David Webb Peoples (story); David Webb Peoples (screenplay). *Hero*. Dir. Stephen Frears. Columbia Pictures Corp., 1992.

Appendix

Aquinas, Thomas. *Summa Theologica of Saint Thomas Aquinas*. Second and Revised Edition, 1920. Online edition. New Advent. 28 Dec 2006 http://www.newadvent.org/summa/2084.htm

Arndt, Michael. *Little Miss Sunshine*. Dir. Jonathan Dayton and Valerie Faris. Fox Searchlight Pictures, 2006.

Berman, John. *Wrath, Lust, and Littering? The New Seven Deadly Sins*. 10 Mar., 2008 ABC News.com 10 Mar. 2008 http://abcnews.go.com/Nightline/story?id=4424390

Carnahan, Matthew Michael. *Lions for Lambs*. Dir. Robert Redford. Andell Entertainment, 2007.

Cassian, John. *The Twelve Books of John Cassian on the Institutes of the Coenobia and the Remedies for the Eight Principal Faults*. 12 June 2000, Order of St. Benedict. 4 Mar 2007 http://www.osb.org/lectio/cassian/inst/index.html

Cook, Peter and Dudley Moore (story); Peter Cook (screenplay). *Bedazzled*. Dir. Stanley Donen. Stanley Donen Films, 1967.

Coppola, Sofia. *Lost in Translation*. Dir. Sofia Coppola. Focus Features, 2003.

Dante Aligheiri. *The Inferno of Dante*. Tr. Robert Pinsky. Farrar, Straus and Giroux, 1997.

Danteworlds. The University of Texas at Austin. 2009. 4 Aug. 2009 http://danteworlds.laits.utexas.edu/index.html

Evagrius Ponticus: Various introductory texts on Virtues and Vices. Fr. Luke Dysinger, St. Andrew's Abbey, 1990. http://www.ldysinger.com/Evagrius/00a_start.htm

Evolution of the Seven Deadly Sins. Evagrius Scholarship Center. 2007 4 Mar 2009 http://www.evagrius.net/articles.php?article_id=19

Gregory the Great, Pope. *Morals on the Book of Job*. Tr. John Henry Parker and J. Rivington. London, 1844. Lectionary Central. 12 Feb 2007 http://www.lectionarycentral.com/GregoryMoraliaIndex.html

Grisham, John (novel); David Rabe (screenplay). *The Firm*. Dir. Sidney Pollack. Paramount, 1993.

Hagy, Jessica. *We're All Going to Hell*. 30, Jan. 2007. Indexed Blog. 12 Mar. 2007 http://thisisindexed.com/2007/01/were-all-going-to-hell/

Heckerling, Amy. *Clueless*. Dir. Amy Heckerling. Paramount, 1999.

Holden, David W. *The Christian Ascetic Tradition of Dejection and Dispondency* 18 Feb. 2007 http://www.ocampr.org/Christian_Ascetic_Tradition_Dejection_Despondency.pdf

Homer (epic); Ethan and Joel Coen (screenplay). *O Brother, Where Art Thou*. Touchstone, 2000.

Homer and Allen Mandelbaum. *The Odyssey of Homer*. New York: Bantam, 1991.

Holy Bible. New Living Translation. Carol Stream, IL Tyndale, 1996.

Hughes, John. *Vacation*. Dir. Harold Ramis. Warner Bros., 1983.

LeCarre, John (novel); Andrew Davies (screenplay). *The Tailor of Panama*. Dir. John Boorman. Columbia Pictures, 2001.

Lewis, C. S. *The Chronicles of Narnia*. Collier, 1976.

Lutz, Karen McCullah and Kristin Smith. *10 Things I Hate About You*. Dir. Gil. Junger. Touchstone, 1999.

Mustane, Dave and David Ellefson. *Seven*. Megadeth. *Risk*. Capitol, 1999.

Panati, Charles. *The Sacred Origin of Profound Things*. New York: Penguin, 1996.

Peoples, David Webb. *Unforgiven*. Dir. Clint Eastwood. Malpaso Productions, 1992.

Pioch, Nicholas. *Bosch, Hieronymous: The Seven Deadly Sins*. Web Museum Paris, 14 Oct. 2002. 15 Jan. 2007 http://www.ibiblio.org/wm/paint/auth/bosch/7sins/

Prudentius (Aurelius Prudentius Clemens). *The Battle for the Soul of Man (Psychomachia)*. Internet Archives Wayback Machine. 30 April 2007 http://web.archive.org/web/20020429135514/http://www.richmond.edu/~wstevens/grvaltexts/psychomachia.html

Rowling, J. K. *The Complete Harry Potter Box Set*. Bloomsbury, 2007.

Rubin, Danny and Harold Ramis. *Groundhog Day*. Dir. Harold Ramis. Columbia Pictures, 1993.

Schaff, Philip, Ed. *A Select Library of Nicene and Post-Nicene Fathers of the Christian Church. Augustin: The Writings against the Manicheans and the Donatists*. Buffalo: The Christian Literature Company, 1887. Online. Google Books http://books.google.com/books?id=9wgNAAAAIAAJ&dq=augustine+define+sin&source=gbs_navlinks_s

Shakespeare, William. *The Taming of the Shrew*. Filiquarian, 2007.

Shakespeare, William. *Twelfth Night*. Simon and Schuster, 2004.

Bibliography

Shyamalan, M. Night. *Lady in the Water*. Dir. M. Night Shyamalan. Warner Bros., 2006.

Smith, Kevin. *Clerks*. Dir. Kevin Smith. View Askew Productions, 1994.

The Seven Deadly Sins. Wikipedia, 4 Aug. 2009. http://en.wikipedia.org/wiki/Seven_deadly_sins

Tolkein, J.R.R. (novel); Walsh, Fran (screenplay) *The Lord of the Rings*. Dir. Peter Jackson. New Line, 2001-2003.

Thorp, Roderick (novel); Job Stuart and Steven E. deSouza (screenplay). *Die Hard*. Dir. John McTiernan. Twentieth Century Fox, 1988.

Walker, Andrew Kevin. *Se7en*. Dir. David Fincher. New Line Cinema, 1995.

Whedon, Joss. *Buffy the Vampire Slayer*. Dir. Fran Rubel Kuzui. Twentieth Century Fox, 1992.

Weiser, Stanley and Oliver Stone. *Wall Street*. Dir. Oliver Stone. Twentieth Century Fox, 1987.

Sinema7

INDEX

28 Days, 35
40-Year Old Virgin, 20-21
Acedia, 62-63
Accepting the past, 84
Addiction, 33-34, 36
Adequacy, 102-103, 107
Adultery, 17, 25, 80
Advice, 107, 119
Aesop, 1, 6
Aggression, 74, 76-78, 82
Altamirano, Cardinal, 113
Alcoholism, 33-35, 40
Amadeus, 89, 94
Ambition, 90, 93-94, 97
American Beauty, 15-16
Animal House, 29, 31
Anthony (*Millions*), 50-51
Aquinas, Thomas, 31, 63
Aristotle, 90
Arrogance, 106, 110-113, 119
As Good as it Gets, 92
August Rush, 69-71
Augustine, 131-133
Austen, Jane, 108-109
Austin Powers: The Spy Who Shagged Me, 31
Avoidance, 60-62
Babette's Feast, 55
Bailey, George, 54
Barbossa, Captain, 56

Batman: The Dark Knight, 114-115
Baylor, Drew (*Elizabethtown*), 100-101
Bell, Ed Tom, 49
Belle, 106, 107
Bennett, Elizabeth (*Pride and Prejudice*), 108
Beauty and the Beast, 106-107
Bible verses
    1 Cor. 1:27, 116
    1 Cor 13, 100, 133
    2 Cor. 9:8, 56
    Acts 17:28a, 103
    Ecc. 9:7-8, 62
    Ecc. 9:11, 95
    Eph. 4:26-27, 81
    Eph. 5:31, 23
    Eze. 25:17, 82
    Gen. 3:23, 23
    Heb. 11:1, 71
    Heb. 12:1b, 37
    James 4:1-3, 44
    Luke 6:38, 55
    Luke 10:27, 70
    Luke 12:15, 54
    Micah 6:8, 120
    Matt. 5:28, 17
    Matt. 6:26, 41
    Phil. 2:3-4, 118
    Proverbs 25:16, 39
    Rom. 12:10b, 55
Big Kahuna, 89, 97-99
The Big Lebowski, 67-68
Billy Madison, 66, 71
Binsfield, Peter, 134
Bitterness, 79-81

Index

Blood Diamond, 51-53
Bluto, 31
Boesky, Ivan, 45
Boone, Herman, 119
Boredom, 32-33, 62, 65
Business, 45, 52, 92, 97-98, 101, 103, 111
Bullying, 78
Burnham, Lester (*The Ref*), 15
Buzz Lightyear, 90-91
Camp Nowhere, 61
Cassian, John, 131-132
Characters, 1-2, 4-5, 7-10, 138-139
Chariots of Fire, 69
Chasseur, Lloyd and Caroline, 79-80
Chigurh, 49-50
Children, 36, 61
Chocolat, 38-39
Christmas, 53-54
Chronicles of Narnia, 139
Church, 38, 40-41, 113-114
Colburn, Claire, 100-101
Competition, 89-90, 95-96
Completion, 22-23, 90, 95-96
Conformity, 90, 95-96
Consumerism, 53-54
Couples, 79-80, 84, 107-108
Cribs, 46
Csikszentmihalyi, Mihaly, 65
Damian, 50-51
Dante, 63, 134, 136-137
Darcy, 108
Deep Impact, 97
Dent, Harvey, 115
The Devil Wears Prada, 109-110

Diamonds, 51-52
Discipline, 37-40
Die Hard, 110-112
Disasters, 112
Dobler, Lloyd, 117-118
Doe, John, 74
The Dude, 67-68
Durden, Tyler, 53, 77
Egotism, 15, 17, 94, 97, 101
Elizabethtown, 100-101
Ellis, Harry, 110-111
Endurance, 37, 40
Entertainment, 6
Evagrius, 131
Existential detectives, 53
Fairness, 91-94
Failure, 91-93, 95-97
Falling Down, 76
Fargo, 46-48
Fat Bastard, 31
Fear, 60, 64
Ferris Bueller's Day Off, 63-64, 71
Fight Club, 53, 77
Flow, 65, 71
Forgiveness, 82, 84-87
Forrest Gump, 102-103
Friendship, 16, 22-24
Frustration, 73-74, 77
Frye, Cameron, 63-64
Gambini, Vincent, 107
Gekko, Gordon, 43, 45
Generosity, 53-55
George, Regina, 78
Gnostic gospels, 136-137

Index

Goethe, 70
Good Will Hunting, 84
Gourmand, 32
Grace, 85-86
Grape, Gilbert, 36-37
Gratification, 40-41
The Great Commandment, 70
The Great Commission, 70
Gregory the Great, 132
Grief, 41, 100
Groundhog Day, 7
Gruber, Hans, 110-111
Guanari, 13-114
Gunderson, Marge, 47-48
Gustafson, Wade, 46-47
Heavy Weights, 36
Heep, Cleveland, 62-63
Heroes, 2, 4
Hitchhiker's Guide to the Galaxy, 65
Hopelessness, 62, 64-65
Hobbits, 116
Hotel Rwanda 85
How Do I Look? 120
Humility, 106, 111, 116-117, 120
Hunting, Will, 84
I Am Legend, 112-113
I Heart Huckabees, 53
Infidelity, 17, 80
It's a Wonderful Life, 54
Idealism, 118
Inferno, 136-137
Jesus, 1, 3, 6, 17, 51, 54-57, 69, 86-87, 92, 120, 127, 144, 146, 150
Jealousy, 90

The Jerk, 44
Jerry Maguire, 13, 22-23
Johnson, Navin, 44
Joker, 114-115
Jules, 82-83
Justice, 93-94, 103
Lady in the Water, 62-63
Law Officers, 47, 49
Laziness, 66
Leaving Las Vegas, 33-34
Lebowski, 67-68
Lecter, Hannibal, 2, 8
Legalism, 38
Lewis, C. S., 38, 117, 139
Liddle, Eric, 69
Little Giants, 95-96
Lions for Lambs, 9
The Lion King, 93-94
Loneliness, 16
The Lord of the Rings, 7, 116
Lost in Translation, 16-17
Love Actually, 17-18
Lundegaard, Jerry, 46-48
McClain, John, 110-111
Mad Magazine, 46
Maguire, Sean, 84
Marriage, 16-17, 21-23, 26, 79
Marvin the Robot, 65
Masculinity, 77
Materialism, 15, 44, 46-47, 51-53
Mathematics, 84
Mean Girls, 78
Megadeth, 139, 155
Melvin, 92

Index

Millions, 50-51
The Mission, 113-114
Moderation, 37, 39
Monogamy, 14, 16
Moonstruck, 14-15, 25
Moss, Llewelyn, 49-50
Mozart, 94-95
Munich, 81
Munny, Will, 82
My Cousin Vinny, 107
Nature, 82
Neibuhr, Reinhold, 83
Neville, Robert, 112-113
No Country for Old Men, 49-50
Obesity, 31, 35-37
The Office, 70
Office Space, 59, 68
O'Shea, Danny & Kevin, 95-96
Others-centered behavior, 99, 101-102
Overeater's Anonymous, 30, 35
Parables, 6
Passion, 23, 25-26
Passive Aggression, 79-80
Patience, 83-84
Paul the Apostle, 1, 8, 133
Pay It Forward, 55
Payback, 81
Persistence, 39-40
Pirates of the Caribbean: The Curse of the Black Pearl, 56
Plato, 133
Pleasantville, 20
Plot, 6-7
Pontius Pilate, 52
Pornography, 18-19

Potter, Mister, 54
Power, 105, 109, 116-117
Pretension, 108-109, 114
Pride and Prejudice, 108-109
Priestley, Miranda, 109
The Princess Bride, 24-25
Prodigal Son, 92
Prostitution, 14, 18-19
Pulp Fiction, 82-83
Purgatorio, 137
Purity, 22, 26
Purpose, 60-62, 69-70, 116
Rage, 76-76, 81-82
Rain Man, 48-49
Ratatouille, 32
Rejection, 96
Relational aggression, 77-78
The Ref, 79-80
Remember the Titans, 119
Regret, 99
Resentment, 90-91, 93
Revenge, 81
Romance22, 24-26
Rudy, 39
Rusesabagina, Paul, 85
Salesmen, 97-98
Salieri, 89, 94
Sam (*Lord Of The Rings*), 101-102
Sarcasm, 111
Say Anything, 117-118
Sayers, Dorothy, 14, 60
Scar (*Lion King*), 93-94
Schadenfreude, 93
Schindler's List, 85

Index

School, 63-64, 66, 70, 76-78
Scrooge, 53
Self-centered, 15, 17, 94, 97, 101
Self-esteem, 63-64, 78, 84
Self-respect, 119-120
Seurat, 64
Sex industry, 18-19
Showalter, Carl (*Fargo*), 47
Sideways, 32-33
Silence of the Lambs, 8
The Sisterhood of the Travelling Pants, 20
Snobbery, 108
Sobriety, 35
Socrates, 133
Spiritual pride, 94-95, 113-114
Sports, 39, 95-96, 119
Spurlock, Morgan, 31, 35
Storytelling, 9
Supersize Me, 31, 35
Supporting role, 101-102, 117-118
Taylor, Evan, 69-70
Temperance, 38
Ten Commandments, 3
Tender Mercies, 40-41
Theme, 9-10
Tokyo, 16
Tommy Boy, 91-92
Toy Story, 90-91
Traffic, 30
Treasure, 56-57
Validation, 95
Vengeance, 81
Venting, 75-76
Villains, 2, 4, 7

Uncle Buck, 70-71
Uncommitted Sex, 21
Unfaithfulness, 14, 18
Unforgiven, 81-82
Van Welker, Dennis (*Camp Nowhere*), 61-62
Virginity, 19-21
A Walk to Remember, 22
Wall Street, 43, 45-46
Weight loss, 36
Weight of glory, 117
Willie Wonka and the Chocolate Factory, 39
What Not to Wear, 120
What's Eating Gilbert Grape, 36-37
When Harry Met Sally, 23-24
Wine, 32-33
Woody, 90-91
Worth, 96-97
Yost, Coach (*Remember the Titans*), 119

Index

MOVIES REFERENCED BY CHAPTER

Introduction & Appendix

Basic Instinct
Bedazzled
Buffy the Vampire Slayer
Groundhog Day
Lady in the Water
Lions for Lambs
Lord of the Rings
Lost in Translation
Se7ven
Silence of the Lambs
The Tailor of Panama
Unforgiven

Lust

40-Year Old Virgin
American Beauty
Independence Day
The In-Laws
Jerry Maguire
Lost in Translation
Love Actually
Moonstruck
Pleasantville
The Princess Bride

Sinema7

The Sisterhood of the Travelling Pants
Trading Places
A Walk to Remember
When Harry Met Sally

Gluttony

28 Days
Animal House
Austin Powers: The Spy Who Shagged Me
Chocolat
Heavy Weights
Leaving Las Vegas
Love Actually
The Meaning of Life
Ratatouille
Sideways
Supersize Me
Tender Mercies
Traffic
Willie Wonka and the Chocolate Factory

Greed

Blood Diamond
Cribs
Fargo
Fight Club
I Heart Huckabees
It's a Wonderful Life
The Jerk
Millions
No Country for Old Men
Pay It Forward

Index

Pirates of the Caribbean: The Curse of the Black Pearl
Rain Man

Sloth

August Rush
The Big Lebowski
Blood Diamond
Camp Nowhere
Chariots of Fire
Failure to Launch
Ferris Bueller's Day Off
Lady in the Water
Millions
Office Space
Hitchhiker's Guide to the Galaxy
Uncle Buck

Anger

Falling Down
Good Will Hunting
House of Sand and Fog
Mean Girls
Munich
The Office (TV)
Pulp Fiction
The Ref
Schindler's List
Se7en
Unforgiven

Envy

Amadeus
As Good As It Gets
The Big Kahuna
Elizabethtown
Forrest Gump
Little Giants
The Lion King
The Lord of the Rings
Tommy Boy
Toy Story

Pride

Batman: The Dark Knight
Beauty and the Beast
The Devil Wears Prada
Die Hard
I am Legend
The Lord of the Rings
The Mission
My Cousin Vinny
Pride and Prejudice
Remember the Titans
Say Anything

MAUREEN'S STORY

Maureen Herring is neither a Film School Graduate nor a Theologian. She is, however, a sinner who likes movies. She has blogged about movies and sin at www.sinema7.net since 2008. She holds an MLIS from the University of Texas at Austin and currently works as a high school librarian. She lives in the Austin, Texas area with her husband and three sons. And, in case you're wondering, she struggles most with anger and sloth.

WHAT'S YOUR STORY?

Join the conversation about the seven deadly sins in movies at:

www.sinema7.net

- View blog posts about new movies
- Read comments from other readers
- Contribute your own thoughts and opinions
- Get news and updates on recent interviews, web links, and events

COMING SOON

THE SINEMA7 SMALL GROUP STUDY GUIDE

Includes movie scene references for each week

The Temptation
- What makes us entertain this sin?
- What need do you think will be met through acting on the temptation?
- What are personal triggers to sin?

The Sin
- What does it look like in action?
- Why don't we always recognize that we're acting on this sin?

The Damage
- How does the damage look when we act on this sin?
- Who is affected?

The Opposing Virtue
- What does behavior that stems from this virtue look like?
- What happens when we practice the opposing virtue?

What Christ Supplies
- How does Christ meet the need this sin suggests it can fulfill?
- How does faith change our focus?

CPSIA information can be obtained at www.ICGtesting.com
Printed in the USA
LVOW031914291211

261513LV00004B/75/P